ALL I REALLY NEED TO KNOW

I LEARNED

FROM WATCHING

STAR

TREK

ALL I REALLY NEED TO KNOW I LEARNED FROM WATCHING STAR TREK

DAVE MARINACCIO

Crown Trade Paperbacks
New York

Published by Crown Trade Paperbacks, 201 East 50th Street, New
York, New York 10022. Member of the Crown Publishing Group.

Random House, Inc. New York, Toronto, London, Sydney, Auckland

Originally published in hardcover by Crown Publishers, Inc., in 1994.

CROWN Trade Paperbacks and colophon are trademarks of Crown
Publishers, Inc.

Manufactured in the United States of America

Design by Lauren Dong

Library of Congress Cataloging-in-Publication Data
Marinaccio, Dave.
    All I really need to know I learned from watching Star Trek /
Dave Marinaccio. — 1st ed.
        p.   cm.
    1. Conduct of life. 2. Star Trek (Television program)—
Miscellanea. 3. Marinaccio, Dave. I. Title.
BJ1581.2.M35 1994   93-44654
158'.1—dc20   CIP

ISBN 0-517-88386-4

10 9 8 7 6 5 4 3 2 1

First Paperback Edition

For
G.A.B.

INTRODUCTION

Iwork in one of the noblest enterprises ever conceived by man, advertising. My work environment is a stress-filled one. About the only thing taken for granted is that today's problems will be completely different from yesterday's. At its best, it can be said that the job offers variety. Unfortunately, it's the same old variety day after day.

In situations of change, it is natural for human beings to look for touchstones. As a human being, I had always sought a center to my life, an example to follow. What I hadn't realized was that I was already following a path into the future. It was pointed out to me at a business meeting.

I was comparing a current problem to something I had watched on television the previous night. I can't recall the particular problem, but I do recall saying, "Well, we could be diplomatic, but as Scotty said on Star Trek last night, 'The best diplomat I know is a fully charged phaser bank.' "

"You turn everything into Star Trek," a coworker responded.

She was right. For years I've related everything in life to Star Trek. But why not? Captain James Tiberius Kirk is the most successful person I've ever observed. He's a great leader, a good manager of people, dedicated, moral, adaptable, at the top of his profession, gets the girls, is well known and respected. There are worse role models.

Most importantly, I was practically a Phi Beta Kappa in Star Trek. As a kid it was my favorite TV show. As an adult, virtually every night after work I would walk in the door, collapse on the couch and hit the remote control. Like most men, the remote control is part of my arm. Unlike most men, I can actually watch an entire program. Just so long as the program is Star Trek.

Anyway, that comment at work helped me discover something I already knew. I realized then that I already know what's necessary to live a meaningful life—that it isn't all that complicated.

ALL I REALLY NEEDED TO KNOW about how to live and what to do and how to be I learned watching Star Trek. These are the things I learned:

• Each person or each species, no matter how alien, has the right to live their lives as they wish. (As long as they're not trying to take over the galaxy or eat you or something.)

• Everyone has a role in life. Sulu is the navigator. Uhura is the communications specialist. Do your own job and the ship will function more smoothly.

• Whatever you are doing, answer a distress call. The most important time to help someone is when they need it.

• If you mess something up, it's your responsibility to make things right again. (Say you disrupt history and cause the Nazis to win World War II. To correct matters, you have to let Joan Collins walk in front of a car even though you're in love with her.)

• The more complex the mind, the greater the need for the simplicity of play.

• If you can keep your head in a crisis you've got a fighting chance.

8

- The unknown is not to be feared. It is to be examined, understood and accepted.
- Close friends become family and family is the true center of the universe.
- End every episode with a smile.
- And lastly, with time and patience you can even learn something from *The Next Generation.*

Everything you need to know is in there somewhere. It may be dressed in some real lame costume. But it's there. Every situation you will face in life has already been faced by the crew of the Starship Enterprise NCC 1701. How to respond to challenge. How to treat your friends. How to pick up girls. How to get ahead on the job. How to run a business. How to bandage a wounded silicon-based life-form. Everything you need to know.

M

any of the things that Star Trek teaches us are unintended. That doesn't make them any less important.

James T. Kirk is the model ship's captain. He's always in fighting shape. He has to be to handle the 2.5 fights per episode. Yet, there it is right in front of us. And right in front of him. A potbelly. Not your five nights a week at Dunkin' Donuts New York City Police Department potbelly. But a very comfortable, let's not push back from the table just yet potbelly.

O.K., on Kirk it looks good. Of course on Kirk everything looks good. From the pointy sideburns to the uniform to the pointy-toed boots. But the potbelly is special. No question about it, it belongs there. Apparently, in the twenty-third century people will be at ease with their bodies.

I'm forty. I work out three or four times a week. Each workout includes 180 sit ups and 40 leg lifts. However, I share every single workout with a potbelly the captain would be proud of.

Spot reduction, the concept of losing weight in a specific area of your body, is impossible. Aerobic activity will burn the fat off a human, just not off the parts a human desires the fat to be burned off of. At least that's what the health and nutrition specialist at the Old Town Athletic Club told me.

Problem is, I'm not fat anywhere else. Just in the stomach.

I figure any reduction would have to take place in that particular spot. Don't ask me why it doesn't.

Incidently, this potbelly thing is really a male problem. Women tend to gain weight in their thighs. A moment on the lips, a lifetime on the hips, as my mother used to say. Without a doubt the greatest inequity between men and women is the simple fact that a man can suck in his gut but a woman can't suck in her thighs.

At any rate, when I see James T. Kirk standing there on the transporter pad, phaser hanging neatly on the side of his slightly bulging waistband, I feel good. And so should you.

Working for an advertising agency means working for many different clients. I've created ads for literally hundreds of products, from Adorn hair spray to McDonald's hamburgers to Weyerhaeuser particleboard. Some companies are dominated by one personality, others develop a corporate culture. From what I have seen, both types of businesses can be successful. The key is that there be clearly identified corporate goals and a decision-making process.

When I worked on Sunkist Orange Soda, they had the most bizarre decision-making process imaginable. After the agency presented the new ideas for television or radio commercials, everyone in the room voted.

Junior writers got one vote. So did the president of the soda company. Obviously, we would stuff as many of our folks into the meetings as possible. Guess what? When the agency had the most people in the room, the agency recommendation stood a solid chance of getting approved. As strange as that process was, at least a decision got made. A lot of client meetings end in analysis paralysis. Nothing ever happens.

While decision-making processes are important, clearly identified corporate goals are more important. In my experience, the best-run companies have a basic philosophy that the people in the company know and understand. Sometimes this philosophy is formalized in a mission statement. Here is the best mission statement I have ever heard.

These are the voyages of the Starship Enterprise. Her five-year mission: to explore strange new worlds, to seek out new life and new civilizations, to boldly go where no man has gone before.

Crew members of the Starship Enterprise know exactly what they are supposed to do. Suppose you are the dumbest person on the ship. How long do you think the mission will last? Five years? Very good. And suppose you encountered a strange new world? What should you do? Explore it, perhaps. There is even an emotion telling you how you should go about exploring it. Boldly.

Now try a simple test. Ask a number of colleagues at your place of work, "What is the single most important thing our company is trying to accomplish?" I've done this myself. Chances are you will receive many different answers. If you run a company, this exercise can be extremely enlightening.

Now ask yourself, if your business encounters a strange new world, what would your dumbest employee do? What if your company encounters a strange new opportunity? Without a basic philosophy, even a business's smartest employees have to improvise when they meet a new or challenging situation.

We could do worse than rewriting the Star Trek mission statement for whatever venture we are on. A simple statement. One that spells out who we are, what we are doing, and how we would like to go about doing it. Maybe even deal with the question of why we are doing it. Make the language exact, the goal specific, and even your worst employee will make you proud.

The Klingons are a rotten lot, immoral, aggressive, ruthless, coarse and generally evil. They are responsible for most of the troubles in this galaxy. They are not like us.

They are a lot like the Russians were in the dreary years of the cold war. They are a lot like the Iraqis were in the dusty days of the war in the Gulf. They are the enemy. All enemies.

Over time, the appearance of the Klingons changed. In the beginning, on the original series, they kind of looked like Mr. Spock—darker skinned than Mr. Spock, but similar.

In *Star Trek: The Motion Picture*, the Klingons looked different. Bony protuberances ran from their noses to their scalps. A fierce enemy had become more fierce for the big screen. What didn't change was the concept of Klingon as enemy. This new face was more faceless. Less individual. Less human. More alien. Easier to hate.

By the time William Shatner kicked Christopher Lloyd (costumed as a Klingon) off the cliff and into the lava flow on the Genesis planet in *Star Trek III*, we had no problem hating the new Klingons as much as the old.

Now there is a Klingon on the bridge of the Enterprise. Enterprise NCC 1701D is the designation of this ship, *Star Trek: The Next Generation* Starship, commanded by Jean-Luc Picard.

Worf is the name of the Klingon, and he is not the hated enemy—he is a beloved member of the crew. Security officer is his job in the twenty-fourth century version of Star Trek. By the twenty-fourth century, Klingons will be our friends.

Nature abhors a vacuum. Drama demands conflict. Ergo, Klingons as enemy have been replaced by the Cardassians. The Cardassians are a rotten lot, immoral, aggressive, ruthless, coarse and generally evil. They are responsible for most of the troubles in this galaxy. They are not like us.

Bottom line. There has to be evil to define good. If a Cardassian shows up as a beloved crew member on *Star Trek: The Generation After the Next Generation*, then a new enemy would appear. (The Romulans have been enemies in both the original series and *The Next Generation*, so they become the odds-on favorite.)

How about no enemies? Only friends. It is possible. If we can solve our differences with the Russians, maybe we don't have to replace them with a new enemy. Maybe we can replace them with a new idea. Think positive. No enemy.

Except, of course, the French.

Of all the things that Star Trek teaches us, the simplest and the most obvious is that mankind's future is in space. Time after time, Captain Kirk gives this little speech about how restless man is. That he is an explorer. That man must have challenge. That he must struggle to survive.

Perhaps this explains why the Enterprise, traveling the universe, exploring countless planets large and small, near and far, never encounters paradise. Utopia doesn't exist in space.

I live in Washington, D.C. We have all your money. Almost every day on the way to work I can watch federal workers digging up flower beds and other federal workers planting new flowers, perhaps pansies. Soon after, other federal workers rip up the recently planted pansies and plant tulips. It's gorgeous.

I sometimes wonder if there are specific government workers who only rip up the flower beds and others who specialize in planting. Or even if there are pansy, tulip and daisy specialists. It's possible.

Meanwhile, other federal workers are mowing the lawns, pruning the trees and washing the sidewalks.

Driving to work in the morning, I often look at the beautiful view I'm afforded just by living in the nation's capital and think about the people in Boise, Idaho, and Hartford, Connecticut, who are paying for my lovely drive. These pretty beds of tulips are your tax dollars at work. And two weeks later, with the tulips still in full bloom, they are ripped out by the ripping crew and the planting crew puts in begonias.

Specialization in this city is close to a disease. We have at least five different police forces that I am aware of. My personal favorite of all the law enforcement divisions is the Secret Service Uniformed Division. Doesn't that strike you as just a little bit funny? If they're the Secret Service, wouldn't the uniform give them away?

On the side of the white cars they drive around America's capital is a shield. The official shield of the Secret Service Uniformed Division. Who is this supposed to be a secret from? Even illiterate criminals can figure out that a car with a shield on the side is a police car.

Even with all your money, all these cops and all these flowers, Washington, D.C., isn't Utopia. Not even close. Truth is, it's a mess. Our murder rate leads the country. You know the story.

Just think of the tremendous amount of money we spend on this place, including money we don't even have. Still no Utopia. And there never ever will be one.

But when I talk to people who don't believe in the space program, they usually feel that we should spend the money here on earth. Let's fix the planet. Take care of the people here. It's a nice thought, but there isn't enough money in the world. Even if there were enough money, watching Congress should teach us there's no way we would ever be able to agree on how to spend it.

How about this. Remember Spain, the place where they had the Olympics? Suppose when Ferdinand and Isabella ran the place they decided not to explore the Atlantic. Instead, they decided to spend the wealth of Spain to fix up Barcelona. To take care of the people there. The Golden Age of Spain would never have happened. Someone other than Columbus would have discovered the New World. Some other country would have reaped the rewards and enjoyed a golden age. And I guarantee you Barcelona would not have become Utopia.

Luckily for you and me, they invested their money in ships of exploration. And their ships of exploration discovered America. I mean, why do you think people speak Spanish in Los Angeles, San Antonio, and Miami? Isabella and Columbus, that's why. We should do the same thing and invest our money in ships of exploration. Spaceships.

Okay. Maybe this is a little preachy. But it is just so damn obvious to me. The same people who think the space program is a waste of money won't leave their houses in the morning until they check the satellite weather channel.

Mankind will go out into space or our species will die

prematurely. I'm too old to be a part of it. I will never stand on Mars. But humans will. As surely as James T. Kirk stands on the bridge of the Enterprise, as surely as Jean-Luc Picard stands on the bridge of the Enterprise D, humans will stand on Mars. We will struggle. We will fight. We will explore.

Face it, even if we created heaven on earth, after a while it would bore us out of our skulls, and we would seek out a new challenge. Space is the ultimate challenge, and that's one thing we cannot resist.

We already have found Utopia. For man, Utopia is endless challenge. And by answering that challenge, maybe we'll find ourselves.

It's absolutely undeniable. True on Star Trek. True in real life. The reason that Captain Kirk gets the girls is that—drumroll, please—he's the captain.

I hate that. Give the fairer sex every chance to look into your soul and see you for the prince you are, and you'll come home from the dance alone. Wear an Armani suit. Make the big bucks. Be the boss. These are the ways to a woman's heart.

As Tony Montana so aptly observed, "First you get the money. Then you get the power. Then you get the women." Yeah, I know that the money part wasn't actually in any episode of Star Trek, but Kirk does drive around in a pretty flashy spaceship.

To be fair, the masculine gender is just as shallow as the distaff side. Men, James T. Kirk included, are suckers for a pretty face. Given the choice of the woman who will make him happy and the woman who will look good on his arm, a man will go for the arm ornament every time.

Once Captain Kirk actually fell in love with a great-looking robot. Hey, she may have been a robot, but what gams. Romancing a robot seems extreme until you take a look at William T. Riker on *The Next Generation*. This guy is after the female of every species in the galaxy. Weird thing is, he isn't interested in human women.

Of the thousand people on the Enterprise D, who has Riker had affairs with? Counselor Deanna Troi, a Betazoid empath, and Ensign Ro Laren, a Bajoran. Also, this guy Riker always takes his vacations on a planet called Risa, which is the Club Med of the twenty-fourth century. So who does he have an affair with on Risa? An alien, of course, who almost takes over the ship and enslaves the Federation.

Listen, Riker, you are very seriously flirting with Space AIDS or something close. Let's show a little restraint. And let's give our earth women a little respect.

But I digress.

So here we are. Women like powerful men. Men like beautiful women. The only real positive thing I can say about this situation is that there are exceptions to every rule.

In the episode where Kirk and Spock went back in time and ended up working in a soup kitchen, Kirk still got the girl. Even as a soup kitchen worker, Kirk carried himself very well. Plus, he was head and heel above the rest of the guys slurping up their dinners. Compared to them, he was a well-dressed, fairly powerful bum with all his teeth.

The lesson here is, be the captain. Or if you're not the captain, groom yourself, dress the best you can, don't slouch and never speak with your mouth full. This is probably good advice for women as well.

Phone just rang. On the other end was a friend with some happy news, a baby boy named Max. The news reinforced something I actually learned before Star Trek.

If you want to have a family, you have to settle down. Fathers and mothers do not trek around the galaxy. They put down roots and face the most demanding challenge of all, the three o'clock feeding.

Skiing is a wonderful sport. Thirty-five is a wonderful age. West Virginia is a wild and wonderful state. The first time I visited West Virginia was when I learned to ski at the age of thirty-five.

Most pro athletes retire by the time they are thirty-five, unless you include golfers as professional athletes. Among other things, thirty-five-year-old humans have lost reflexes and flexibility during their excursion through life. That fact is painfully apparent to athletes who continually use their reflexes and flexibility. The more sedentary masses, however, don't truly realize that these abilities are no longer available to be called on when needed. Skiing, I was soon to find, is an activity that tests both the reflexes and flexibility of its participants.

One might reasonably ask why a thirty-five-year-old man would take up skiing. Two reasons. The obvious, a twenty-five-year-old girlfriend. And second, a philosophy gleaned from my favorite television program, that the unknown is not to be feared, it is to be examined, understood and accepted.

Undoubtedly, this philosophy can lead to strained ligaments, but it's a heck of a lot of fun. Besides, when did Captain Kirk ever back down from a challenge, especially when a woman was involved?

So it came to be that I was standing with two boards strapped to my feet, slippery snow beneath and a friend shouting instructions at my side.

Most ski slopes have a bunny hill. This is an extremely gentle slope where fledgling skiers cannot build up enough momentum to seriously hurt themselves or others. I believe the name *bunny hill* comes from the Latin *snow bunny*, which is a young woman who cannot ski but enjoys wearing very colorful and attention-getting ski clothes.

Allison, my friend, had given me the instructions for the snowplow. This is a method of skiing slowly and under control. Pointing your skis toward each other (but not crossing the tips), you head downhill. The sides of your skis, which are angled slightly forward, will pile up snow, like a plow, and keep you from gaining speed.

Allison had not given me the instructions for stopping. And there was a compelling reason for stopping a few feet ahead: Japanese ski school. Ten short, dark-haired Japanese men standing side by side on skis. I was approaching from the side.

It wasn't a question of *if* I would hit the line, it was a question of how many Japanese ski students I would knock over. Strictly a matter of physics.

Any Physics 101 student will tell you that speed times mass equals momentum. Let's calculate. Including the ski equipment, long johns, sweaters, etc., I weighed about 195 pounds. My speed was probably 1.5 miles per hour. Therefore, I figured I was going to knock over two Japanese ski students.

As the last few feet between myself and the inevitable disappeared, I screamed, "Look out! Look out! LOOK OUT!" The noise caught the attention of the man nearest me. He turned toward me with a puzzled look on his face.

Like in a nightmare where the action takes place in slow motion, I languidly hit the gentleman with the puzzled expression on his face. He fell in equally slow motion into the gentleman next to him. In the sixties, we didn't believe in the domino theory. Now I had vivid proof. Skier number two fell into skier number three.

As the skiers in line were novices, none of them knew how to get out of the way. One little, two little, three little skiers. Skier number three gave me hope as he momentarily regained his balance before he toppled into skier number four.

I now realized the name *bunny hill* comes from the English *Benny Hill*, meaning thirty minutes of nonstop slapstick action.

The event continued to unfold, and I was still moving. So this is the snowplow. Bodies were piling in front of my skis. If only I had the reflexes and flexibility of your average professional golfer.

Mercifully, the fifth skier in line was stopped from falling by the sixth. A hush filled the nearby surroundings. No one spoke. Eyes did all the talking needed. They said, "You are a total idiot."

We managed to untangle ourselves. I put my tail between my legs and my skis under my arms and walked away.

Allison, my friend, wanted to tell me what I had done wrong. Listening was not a strong point of mine at this particular moment. Leaning the skis against the lodge, I retired to the bar.

Skiing is a wonderful sport. Forty is a wonderful age. Over the past five years, skiing has become a favorite pastime. Colorado and Vermont have been added to my skiing itinerary since that first trek to West Virginia. An unknown experience has been examined, understood and accepted. Skiing has become a wonderful part of my life.

I hope someday to ski in Europe. I plan on avoiding Japan.

Kirk is a military man. His method of dealing with conflict is to meet it straight-on. The problem with this approach is evident on almost every episode.

By the third commercial, the ship is in danger, the crew is in danger and there is no easy or apparent way out. Then it gets worse. Before you know it, Mr. Scott is screaming over the communicator that the ship is going to blow up.

Good drama, but hardly the way to go about your day-to-day business. A more rational approach, and one occasionally used on the show, is the tactic Kirk tried in the episode called "Space Seed." Ricardo Montalban, portraying Khan, has just been thawed out from a frozen state and Kirk wants to find out more about him. Cleverly, Kirk invites Khan to dinner and lets Spock put Khan on the hot seat with some very pointed questions.

This is exactly the format used by many Italian parents to teach their children how to deal with conflict. The Italian parent in this scenario is my father, Alexander Teresio

Marinaccio. My father would sit us down around a large wooden table. Over the course of the next hour, every family member would confront every other family member. Your actions, your personality, even your clothes were called into question.

Volume was extremely important. The louder, the better. Alliances were formed and broken in minutes. The experience was intense. We called this exercise dinner.

Those dinner-table discussions served me well in future years. They taught me to stand on my own two feet, to make my case and hold my ground. They also taught me that there are times for repose during an argument—I mean discussion—times to just sit back and watch.

Letting someone else carry the action for a while allows you to rest, observe and analyze. As Yogi Berra, the great Yankee catcher, once said, "You can observe a lot, just by watching." Which is the tactic Kirk employed with Khan.

The larger lesson is not to run away from conflict. In my home, running away from conflict would have led to missing dinner every night, which in turn would have led to starvation. Besides, conflict can't be avoided in life and shouldn't be. In conflict there is information and growth. In conflict there is, or can be, profit. Whatever doesn't kill you makes you stronger. It doesn't matter whether you use Kirk's straightforward approach or my father's very loud approach. Stand your ground.

Captain Kirk isn't married. Neither am I. Both of us enjoy the company of women. We both chase them and occasionally catch them. But neither of us have found that one girl.

The captain is married to his ship, the Enterprise NCC 1701. He truly loves the ship. He is obsessed with it. There is no room in his life for another love.

I've remained single for a different reason. Sure, I spend a lot of time at work. But I've never been accused of being married to my job. No, work isn't the reason for my long bachelorhood.

The real reason I've never taken a bride is my brothers and sisters. This isn't blame, it's an explanation. Imagine if you will a family with three boys and three girls.

The oldest, Alan, met Betty and married her.

Amber was the next oldest. She met and wed Harry.

Alice Jean met Arthur and they tied the knot.

I was next oldest. Let's skip me.

Barbara was second youngest, still is. She met David and they got hitched.

Mark, the baby, walked down the aisle with Karen.

A small number of sons, daughters, nieces, nephews, cats, dogs and parrots followed. And they all lived happily ever after.

I'm not kidding. All my brothers and sisters fell in love, got married and stayed married. Stayed in love, too.

In a country where one out of two marriages end in divorce, all my siblings have beaten the odds. I'm not saying they have perfect marriages or they haven't experienced tough times. They just picked the right person and made a lifetime commitment.

Needless to say, this is a pretty high standard to live up to. And it puts me under tremendous pressure. If I don't make a lifetime match, I spoil the whole set. Divorce isn't an option for me. Imagine yourself in a similar circumstance.

Since none of the major Star Trek characters ever got married, there are no other role models for me to look to. Well, that isn't exactly true. Mr. Spock got married in one episode. But Vulcans are like salmon. They have to go back to the place of their family origins to marry. Also, they get engaged at the age of eleven or so, then marry at a predetermined time in the future. When Vulcan blood begins to boil and causes a very high fever, it's time to find a justice of the peace. On closer examination, maybe Vulcans aren't really very much like salmon. But they aren't very much like humans, either. And that's my point.

When Spock did get married, the whole thing turned out to be pretty much of a mess. The marriage wasn't even consummated, so it really doesn't count. So where does that leave us?

It leaves Kirk with the ship, Alan with Betty, Amber with Harry, Alice Jean with Art, Barbara with Dave, and Mark with Karen.

And it leaves me right where I started. Maybe someday?

We haven't talked about Mr. Spock very much to this point. The enormous popularity of the Spock character was one of the major reasons for the success of Star Trek. Half logical Vulcan, half emotional human. I don't want to say Mr. Spock is smart, so I'll just describe him as the thinking man's Albert Einstein.

For all his intelligence, Spock is troubled. Completely torn in two between his conflicting halves. Mr. Spock pretends to be perfectly adjusted. He is, in fact, perfectly schizophrenic.

Regular viewers of the show know that Mr. Spock is putting up a front, a facade that denies his basic nature. He elevates his Vulcan heritage while hiding from his human side. As likable as the character is, Spock is basically dishonest. He just isn't being himself.

This can be a tremendous problem unless you happen to be in advertising. In advertising the last person you need to be is yourself. In fact, being a schizophrenic is a definite advantage.

One day you're writing a perfume ad that is supposed to appeal to young women. The next day you have to convince an elderly investor to move his individual retirement account from a mutual fund to certificates of deposit. You have to put yourself in so many different pairs of shoes it's like working at Florsheim.

Once I tried to impress a new boss by walking into his office and identifying myself by saying, "Hi, I'm Dave Marinaccio and I'm a schizophrenic."

The new creative director looked up from his desk and replied, "That makes four of us."

While this type of behavior is a positive boon in my professional life, even admen go home at night—most nights. And at home, denying your basic nature is not a very good idea. Just look at the tormented Spock.

Ask any fan of Star Trek to recall their favorite moments of the series and inevitably one of those moments will be when Spock smiled. Or the time Spock fell in love, or the time Spock cried. Or when Spock crossed the line and acted human. I think we enjoy this so much because these are the times when Spock lets his guard down and is just being himself. This is the real Spock.

My favorite scene of this type occurs in "Amok Time" when Spock enters sick bay and discovers Captain Kirk isn't dead. Spock is ecstatic. He thought he had killed the captain earlier in the episode. After catching himself in a huge smile, the Vulcan first officer regains his emotionless mask.

Doctor McCoy, however, has witnessed Spock's lapse and begins to needle him. Kirk comes to the rescue. "C'mon, Mr. Spock," Kirk says. "Let's go mind the store." Kirk and Spock turn away from McCoy and walk out of sick bay together.

There are two great lessons in one scene. The obvious lesson, taught but not learned by Mr. Spock, is just to be yourself. It feels good. Or to put it more poetically, to thine own self be true. True for me, true for you, true for the Vulcan first officer.

The second, more subtle lesson is delivered by the captain. Kirk knows Spock lives in a world of self-deception, but he lets him ride. Kirk could have ganged up with McCoy to confront Spock. Instead he supports Spock. Gives him a way out when he needs one.

There are plenty of times when Kirk implores Spock to let his human side out, but not now. Not when it will hurt him. Not when he's vulnerable. For Captain Kirk, part of being himself is being a good friend.

No one on the Enterprise has very much stuff. You know, stuff. The things we all accumulate over the course of our lives. Sure, there isn't that much room on the ship to accumulate stuff. Even the captain's quarters are about half the size of a room at a Motel 6. We're talking small.

But I think there's something a little bigger going on here. Mainly that possessions are not the way to judge if a life is full. People don't need to fill their lives with things. What the humans on the Enterprise have are full lives, interesting lives.

During the 1980s, possessions were king. A favorite bumper sticker of mine that became very popular in the recently passed decade said "Whoever dies with the most toys wins." The eighties were the "me" decade. While addressing the stockholders of a fictitious company in the movie *Wall Street*, Michael Douglas pronounced the eighties credo: Greed is good, greed works. Let us all bow our heads in remembrance of the values of the 1980s. And say a little prayer that they never return.

Excessiveness marked the eighties, but the idea of collecting and having a lot of stuff has been around for a long time. Keeping up with the Joneses was a favorite pastime in the

1950s. Long before that, Herbert Hoover won the White House by promising a chicken in every pot.

Let me tell you a strange little story. When I was growing up, I had a friend who had a dream. No, not that dream, a head-on-the-pillow type of dream. His dream was this. He went to a furniture store to pick out furniture for his apartment.

Paul, my friend, is a nice guy. Even-tempered. Good musician. Kind of boring. Paul dreamt he was buying furniture. Some folks don't even think about buying furniture when they're in a furniture store. Paul had this dream when we were in high school. High school!

High school is anguish. Everything is magnified. Information is pouring in from infinite angles. Bad advice and good advice are indistinguishable. Idealism abounds. Life is exploding. And Paul is dreaming about buying furniture. You know, stuff. Ohhh, that's a very nice Chippendale chair, but will it fit with my Bauhaus-influenced Barcelonas?

I bet his living room looks very nice today.

On the Enterprise, the choices are much more limited. Because there is less room, the things that people have say much more about them. Kind of like your dorm room in college. Everyone had the same bed, the same desk, the same closet. Individuality was expressed in your choice of wastepaper basket and posters. If you walked in a room and saw a large picture of Barry Manilow in concert, WATCH OUT!

Captain Kirk's quarters made the most appearances on the show. Very Spartan were Kirk's quarters. But predictable for a military man.

Of greater interest is the way Mr. Spock's room was decorated. Any third-rate fortune-teller would have felt right at home in his digs. The light was always very low, and there were screens and muted colors throughout. In the back was a Vulcan meditation vault. For all the logic and rationality of

29

Spock's day-to-day existence, in his room mysticism and spirituality were the fashion.

Spock also kept a musical instrument called a lyrette. A true renaissance man (or renaissance alien, as the case may be). During one episode he played the lyrette; in another, he sang a song about "bitter dregs." This was the low point of the entire Star Trek series.

In Spock's defense, many of us save the musical instruments of our youth and occasionally have the courage to play them. Fortunately, you and I don't have to perform in front of a national television audience. I no longer own the bass guitar I took lessons for in high school. What remains from that experience is the love of rock and roll that bass guitar helped me develop.

Which brings us back to stuff versus experience. What the voyages of the Enterprise are about is *knowledge*. What the voyage of life is about is the same. Back when the Russians and Americans were racing to the moon, Neil Armstrong and Buzz Aldrin got there first. They returned with a bunch of moon rocks for scientists to examine.

Compared with the experience of going to the moon, those moon rocks are just rocks. Somewhere in a laboratory those rocks are being examined, while all around the world imaginations are fired with the knowledge that the moon is a place we can actually go.

Given the choice, I would rather have an adventure than stuff. My adventures are scuba diving in the Cayman Islands and hang gliding in North Carolina. Cashing in those vacations could probably have gotten me a nicer car or Barcelona chairs. For me, it's no contest. Although I may not get to go where no man has gone before, I'll happily settle for going someplace where I've never gone before. And living a fuller and more interesting life.

Traveling around the galaxy at warp five, which I understand to be two hundred and fifty-six times the speed of light, you pick up a thing or two. One is that humans are imperfect. It doesn't take a degree in quantum physics to leap to this conclusion. Still, bounding around the galaxy and discovering other species provides a mirror for looking at ourselves. Aliens have strengths and weaknesses, just like us. And each time the Enterprise encounters a new life-form, we have a new measuring stick.

Many of these alien species have much to be admired. Some have no trace of war. Others are rational. Still others have immune systems that prevent them from ever being infected by disease. Some are simple gatherers, taking no more than they need from their planet, living lives of complete contentment. Much like Elsie, the Borden cow.

Strikingly, none of these species are perfect, either. In each society there is a flaw. The Gideons, who are immune to death and disease, suffer a terrible overpopulation problem. The simple worshippers of Vaal have the IQs of eggplants.

And what does this measuring stick show us? What is our greatest imperfection? I think it is this. We are attracted to the very things that harm us the most.

An example. Human beings, *Homo sapiens*, folks, us, get

addicted to heroin. We don't get addicted to health food. We don't get addicted to school. We don't get addicted to building a better life and loving each other. We get addicted to a drug that turns us into drooling idiots. A drug that eventually turns normal healthy human beings into criminals. Because the only way one can afford the wonderful feeling this insidious drug provides is by stealing.

A second example. Chocolate. I love it. Chances are, so do you. It is a multimillion-dollar industry. Perhaps more. Give a child the option of eating chocolate or broccoli and the child will pick chocolate every time. So would former president George Herbert Walker Bush.

I strongly expect broccoli, which is good for a human being, would finish far behind on a list that included cotton candy, M&M's, ice cream and hot fudge. All of which are not especially good for you.

Take the potato. The potato is good for you, but it can be made into something that has almost no nutritional value and is loaded with grease—potato chips. Which do you prefer, the potato or the chip?

To continue. Imagine the worst possible thing you can do for your skin. You got it, tanning. It causes skin cancer— CANCER!

Now, plan a vacation. Florida, anyone? How about Cancun? What should we do when we get there? How about spreading a towel on the beach and letting the strongest rays of the sun reaching the face of the planet turn us a deep brown? Ahhh, now that's living.

Is it any wonder that our most enduring method of solving problems is warfare? If you have cable TV, you can watch war all night. It's captivating. We love it. In fact, the greatest sacrifice a human male can make—coming soon to human females everywhere—is to give his life for his country.

Don't misread this. There are many brave people who have fought to make us free, who have honored principles with the last full measure of devotion. But in most cases, warfare could be avoided. It is a failing of the species to which we belong. It is usually the last refuge of wounded pride or some equally meaningless posturing.

The amazing part of all this is that humans have progressed so far, that such a destructive species flourishes. And we do. We keep on keeping on. Humans are drawn like moths to the flame that will burn and kill us. And we draw strength from the experience. We survive.

At its core the question becomes, is man basically good or evil? That is a question for the ages. From what I've seen we must be good. With all these horrible tendencies—our affection for drugs, chocolate, war, Barry Manilow music—we still reach for the stars. If we can prevail against these, then maybe life is a test we can pass. And maybe, just as Star Trek predicts, a better day is coming.

Beam me up, Scotty. If there's a single phrase that has moved from Star Trek to general usage, it's "Beam me up, Scotty." That's because this phrase works in almost any situation.

For example: You've forgotten your spouse's anniversary. At the moment your spouse discovers your blunder, you simply say, "Beam me up, Scotty." In an instant Mr. Scott will beam you directly to the bridge and out of trouble.

Maybe not. If you've seen Scotty lately, you know there's a good chance he's in the mess hall and not the transporter room.

To me, "Beam me up, Scotty" is just a way of saying the world is beyond my control. Humans are used to this condition. Relatively speaking, few things are really in our control.

In the house where I grew up there was a small plaque near the coat closet. It read, "God grant me the serenity to accept the things I cannot change, courage to change the things I can, and wisdom to know the difference." That's the eloquent way to say we are rarely masters of our own fate.

There is a popular and stupider way to say the same thing: "Sh*t Happens."

I couldn't imagine putting a "Sh*t Happens" bumper sticker on my car. When I see a car with that bumper sticker, I think the driver of the vehicle should be fined. Or have his or her mouth washed out with soap. Car bumpers are a public forum, and vulgarity doesn't belong on public display. Not as long as there are children riding around in other cars.

Besides, "Sh*t Happens" is an excuse. It's whining. Crying, "It's not my fault," like some big baby.

You don't get to pick the situations you are dealt in life. But you get to decide how you react. Individuals decide for themselves how they respond to situations. Star Trek usually shows us a positive path to take. The basic philosophy of the show is that man is improving, getting better. Even though there will always be circumstances beyond our control, we control ourselves.

What "Beam me up, Scotty" means is that you realize an event is beyond your control but you're going to react with a sense of humor and then move on. After Scotty beams Kirk out of trouble on Star Trek, the captain regains control and comes out on top. Being beamed up is the captain's way of taking a time-out. We can't always take a time-out in life when we want, but we can always call out for Lieutenant Commander Scott. The act of calling Scotty is a mental time-out. It gives you a second of relief to regain control. Then, like the captain, you're ready to move on. And win.

I have a bachelor of science degree in home economics from the University of Connecticut. It's a little unusual for a man. My major was child development and family relations. Psychology and education were my split minor.

How I came to get this degree is a study in how *not* to get a college education. My first semester in college I achieved—definitely the wrong word—a cumulative average of 0.7 on a scale of 4.0. Semester two my average zoomed up to 1.2.

College was fantastic. I truly enjoyed it. In fact, I truly enjoyed it a little too much. To prevent myself from flunking out, in my remaining semesters I took all the same courses as my girlfriend. As she passed, so did I. After a couple of semesters on this system I almost—almost—made the honor roll.

Her major was child development and family relations. Her degree is from the school of home economics. Since they couldn't give her two degrees, I got one. I owe it to her.

The roots of my educational demise began in high school. Up to my sophomore year, gradewise, I was fairly average. The year was 1967, now known as the Summer of Love. I grew my hair, short by today's standards but noticeable in the mid-sixties, and I started hanging out with an intellectual crowd, wearing blue jeans and tied-dyed T-shirts and attending rock concerts.

As you might imagine, this thrilled my parents no end. Dad was especially upset when I decided to paint a peace symbol on the back of my hand.

My senior year I began a precipitous drop. Not quite tune in, turn on and drop out, but I skipped a lot of school and began to hang around the streets panhandling with my friends. Our joke greeting to each other was "Peace. Love. Bell-bottoms. Got any spare change?"

Passersby would occasionally ask if we were hippies. "No!" we'd say. "Never met one." Just hated the label, I guess. We weren't sure what we were, but we didn't consider ourselves hippies.

I was accepted to college mostly because of decent SAT scores. At UConn my hair got longer. I really didn't do anything, it just grew. When you stop cutting your hair, everyone asks if you are growing your hair. The obvious answer is yes. Everyone is growing their hair. And in college in the early seventies everyone was not cutting their hair, too.

One evening, while visiting in my girlfriend's dormitory, Crandall B, I met some of the young women who lived on her floor. One of the women wore a button on her shirt. It read "Star Trek Lives."

By this time, Star Trek had been off the air for a number of years. It was not yet into wide syndication. Very few reruns were on the cableless airwaves, and the home VCR was still a distant dream. So most of us had not seen the Enterprise in a long time.

It was an exciting moment. This particular young woman had attended a Star Trek convention in New York City, and ten thousand people had joined her. We talked extensively about our favorite episodes. I asked a million questions about the convention. Through this conversation, both of us felt as if we were part of something larger. What would become the Star Trek phenomenon was just beginning, and both of us knew it would grow.

Soon I would be in Star Trek overdrive. Countless reruns filled my afternoons and nights. Shown virtually any scene from any episode, I would be able to recall the entire story of the episode and quote interesting lines of dialogue verbatim.

I became aware that any member of a landing party wearing a red shirt would not survive to the next commercial. I knew that Mark Lenard, the actor who portrayed Spock's father, had been a Romulan captain on a previous episode. I knew that Nurse Chapel had played the part of Number One in the first failed Star Trek pilot.

My abilities grew until only a few seconds of any scene would reveal the entire episode to me. Like Gary Lockwood in the episode titled "Where No Man Has Gone Before," I keep learning and learning. Still I watched. Many of my friends suffered the same affliction.

Suddenly a new word appeared. A word that was meant to describe us all. The word was *Trekkie*. "Are you a Trekkie?" I was asked. "No. Never met one," I would reply. Just hated the label, I guess.

By the end of my college career, I had a degree in home economics. And something that I would carry with me for the rest of my life. A love of the captain and crew of the Starship Enterprise. Fatefully, no longer did I have the love of that resolute young woman who got me through the University of Connecticut. But that is a different story.

Star Trek II: The Wrath of Khan opens with academy cadet Kirstie Alley taking a test. The test is called the Kobayashi Maru, the no-win scenario. Bodies fly all over the screen when Alley, portraying the Vulcan character Lieutenant Saavik, fails the test.

Failing the no-win scenario isn't so bad. As you might have suspected, you can't win.

Here's the test. The Kobayashi Maru is a transport ship that has inadvertently crossed into Klingon space. Klingons attack the ship and are well on their way to destroying it. Alley's ship receives a distress call revealing this information. Hundreds of people on the Kobayashi Maru will lose their lives if her ship takes no action. If she chooses to cross into Klingon space to attempt a rescue, then she is fair game for the Klingons, who far outnumber her.

Kinda like getting into the left lane on a city street. You may move very quickly for a couple of blocks, but just one car turning left in front of you can stop you cold. Sitting there waiting for the lane to clear, you give back all the time and distance you've gained. Cars you zoomed past are now passing you.

Stay in the right lane and you pass no one, moving glacially toward your destination while the left lane breezes by. This is the no-win scenario. The Kobayashi Maru.

Trying to save the transport turned out to be Alley's downfall. Quickly swarmed over by the Klingons, her ship was blasted out of the heavens.

Character is what the test measures. How does one react to a situation where there is no satisfying outcome? Unlike presidential elections, character counts when one must pilot a starship.

Later in the movie, we find out that one person has actually won the no-win scenario. The only cadet in Starfleet Academy history to successfully cross into Klingon space and rescue the Kobayashi Maru? James Tiberius Kirk.

Kirk managed to change the programming of the computer that ran the Kobayashi Maru simulation. Whether this was cheating or original thinking is open to debate. Unlike the rest of us, Kirk never had to face the no-win scenario.

The opposite of the no-win scenario is, obviously, the no-lose scenario. This is rare on planet earth. Unless your name is Richard Gere. Richard faces the extremely difficult choice of staying at work and doing love scenes with Debra Winger, Lauren Hutton and Jodie Foster or going home to his wife, Cindy Crawford. Oh, yeah, Richard is also a millionaire.

If you're like the remainder of the world (i.e., those of us who are not Richard Gere), you probably face the no-win scenario every day.

Fathers and mothers have to decide whether they should take their son, who wants to stay home and play baseball, to visit the aunt who really wants to see him. College students must choose between easy courses that will improve their grades or tough courses that will improve their minds. Professionals wake up sick and wonder whether to go to work at half speed and infect everyone in the office or stay home and fall behind. Television networks always put the best shows on opposite each other.

So what is the value of this concept? It tells you what is really important. Difficult choices expose how we truly feel. What we believe deep inside.

Crossing the neutral zone to rescue the ship shows a willingness to take a chance and a little recklessness. Ignoring the distress call shows an appreciation of what you have, a reluctance to risk what you already hold. Each choice a person makes reveals something about the person. The no-win choice cannot be faked. Consequences are great for any option.

Life, unlike the Kobayashi Maru, is not a simulation. You may not recognize the no-win scenario when it happens in your life. You may not want to. Sometimes when unpleasant things befall us, we simply deny them.

The lesson I've taken from the Kobayashi Maru is not to avoid the unpleasant in life. Make a decision and learn from the consequences, good or bad. After bad experiences, I try to grade my performance. Examining my behavior changes it. Hopefully makes it better.

There's also a lesson from Captain Kirk. When faced with a potential no-win scenario, try something new. Reprogram the situation. Find a way out. Don't stop trying. And maybe, with original thinking, you too can win the no-win scenario.

It's hard to infer Star Trek's opinion of pets. No one on the Enterprise has one. No one on the NCC 1701 Enterprise, that is. On the Enterprise NCC 1701D, the starship of *The Next Generation,* Commander Data has a cat. Also, in the captain's ready room there is an aquarium with . . . fish? Something that looks like fish, anyhow. Either way, whatever is in the bowl behind

Picard's desk really doesn't qualify as a pet. And when you consider that Data isn't human—he's an android—no one on the Enterprise D has a pet, either.

On the original series, tribbles were kept as pets in "The Trouble with Tribbles" episode. Tribbles were basically furry little balls that purred and had an incredible propensity to breed. Sort of like rabbits on fertility drugs. Everyone on the ship loved them. Kirk eventually kicked them off the ship because there were so many of them they were fouling up the machinery.

Let's give the crew the benefit of the doubt. Maybe the reason there are no cats or dogs on the Enterprise is the same reason I don't have a pet. It simply wouldn't be fair to the animal.

Size alone would dictate that any animal on board would have to be fairly small, like a city cat. You know, those cats who live their whole lives in six-hundred-square-foot apartments on the eighteenth floor of New York City high-rises.

What kind of life is that for a cat? I've known such cats. Watching them look longingly at birds that fly past the window, it's obvious this is not a natural state.

What's really crazy is when people living in similar conditions own one-hundred-and-fifty-pound German shepherds. I have no doubt these folks love their dogs. But it's not fair to the animal.

The other day I heard an incredible idea. Virtual reality for city pets. Fit a dog with a computerized helmet and transform your living room into the Serengeti. Of course, until the virtual reality pooper scooper is invented, a real mess could ensue.

Back on the Enterprise, the crew has an erratic schedule. What with fighting Romulans, exploring strange new worlds and examining gaseous anomalies, who has time for feeding, walking and scratching bellies?

Pets care for us because we care for them. If you can't care for a pet, you shouldn't have one.

I'd love to have a dog. I almost got a couple of parakeets. Even had them named, Sutter and Tidrow. Bottom line was, I didn't think I could care for the birds. Maybe I'll settle for fish. Or something that looks like fish.

The unknown is not to be avoided. It is to be examined, understood and accepted. Fear should be treated exactly the same way. As a young man, I had an aversion to flying in airplanes. The most apt description would be that I was a white-knuckle flyer.

My first airplane ride didn't occur until I was twenty-two years old. Eastern Airlines took me from Hartford to Chicago. I enjoyed flying, face plastered to the window, until a Cleveland flight from Chicago a couple of years later.

Before the plane could get above the weather, we flew through a thunderstorm. Someone once said flying is hours of boredom interrupted by seconds of sheer terror. This particular ascent was half an hour in a Veg-O-matic. I realized something was up when the pilot instructed the flight attendants to return to *their* seats and strap in.

After this experience, flying became less enjoyable. The ride to Cleveland had shaken more than the plane. It had shaken my faith. Clearly, something had to be done.

To me the solution seemed obvious. Embrace your fears. Make a friend of horror. Get back up on the horse. Once more into the breach. Yes, my solution to being a white-knuckle flyer was to become a skydiver.

Once you've fallen through the sky in a jumpsuit, I reasoned, being in a plane will seem very solid indeed. A young woman who was a friend of mine agreed to join me in this adventure.

So it came to be that one bright Saturday morning we headed to Roosevelt Field in Warm Springs, Georgia, and a date with destiny. Atlanta Air Sports was to indoctrinate us in the ways of parachute jumping. The day's activities had been explained to us over the phone. Arrive early and sit through two hours of classroom instruction, which would be followed by a couple of hours of ground school. Finally we would be taken aloft to make a jump.

During the classroom session I noticed a problem. Our instructor, Tim, seemed much more interested in instructing my female companion than he did me. She received a high level of personal instruction from Tim. I received little attention at all.

My concern was not jealousy. I neither dated nor was I sexually interested in my friend. No, my concern was for my life.

Still, I wanted to jump very much. But questions were forming in my mind, foremost of which was "Is this a good idea?"

About this time we learned what to do if our parachute didn't open. In fact, we learned about the multiple ways our parachutes could fail to open. A skydiver falling through the clouds at an increasing rate of acceleration must be able to identify the type of malfunction that has befallen his chute. I knew exactly what I would do if I experienced a malfunction. I would die.

As the morning turned to afternoon, our class moved outside. On the tarmac we watched jumpers climb into a Cessna 182. They were ferried to eight thousand feet and then left the plane. From eight thousand feet a jumper can stay in free fall for about twenty-five or thirty seconds. From the ground, jumpers look like dots. Slowly the dots get arms and legs. "Open the chute," your brain starts to repeat as the jumpers get closer. In an instant, the skydivers are under canopy and float to the ground.

Watching this ritual time after time built our confidence. Jumpers went up and jumpers came down. Seemed to be enjoying themselves, too.

The camaraderie was contagious. "You're gonna love it," more than one jumper said to us. Occasionally a jumper would come over and observe us practicing. "Hit the back of your thigh on your PLF," one said. (A PLF is a parachute landing fall.) It takes the shock out of hitting the ground, which you do at pretty high speed even with a fully deployed parachute.

Finally Tim thought we were ready. In front of the plane we stopped for a photograph. I managed a smile.

Perhaps you've heard the question, "Why would anyone jump out of a perfectly good airplane?" One look at this plane gave me the answer. Jumping was probably a good idea if this bucket of bolts actually got us into the air.

We were ferried up to our jump height of three thousand feet. A static line was attached to my parachute. This line would automatically pull the ripcord as I fell from the plane. Tim opened the door of the plane.

Stick your head out the window when your car is going sixty miles an hour. Imagine gas and oil are pouring out of your engine, which is also producing five times as much noise as usual. Now imagine your car is three thousand feet above the ground. Magnify all the above with fear for your life. Lastly, leap from the car. That's skydiving.

"Feet out the door. Stand on the strut. Jump! Jump! JUMP!" The third time Tim yelled, "Jump," I did.

My mind went blank as I stepped into the air. At the end of the static line was the static of my brain waves. The next few moments do not exist in my memory.

The chute opened and I came out of a coma. Silence. An amazing view and silence greeted my return to the land of the living. A tremendous sense of calm filled me. Here, at 2,980 feet, I felt at ease, I felt happy.

Slowly I came to earth. Lazily I drifted downward. Nearer to the ground things started to speed up. The ground rushed up and reminded me to get ready for a PLF. The experienced jumpers had predicted my PLF would be a disaster. Newcomers just never get them right. This newcomer did a perfect PLF. I daisy-chained my parachute and walked one hundred yards back to the takeoff point.

Wow, did I feel good.

I continued jumping until they took me off the static line and let me pull my own ripcord. That summer I made fifteen jumps. Since then I have made numerous airplane trips.

Turbulence still gets my attention when I fly, and occasionally I feel a little nervous. But I feel good about myself. I examined, understood and accepted something that had scared me. I don't skydive anymore, but I wouldn't trade the experience for anything.

To say any episode of Star Trek was the best is to take away from the others. Certain episodes did make a deeper impression than others. And some fired the imagination, giving them a life beyond the show.

One such episode was "Mirror, Mirror." Most people remember this episode as the one where Mr. Spock had a beard. What happens is the transporter, a finicky piece of

45

machinery, is scrambled by an ion storm. When Kirk, Uhura and McCoy are rematerialized, they end up in a parallel universe. Back on the Enterprise, a Kirk, McCoy and Uhura from the parallel universe rematerialize.

Normally when people from parallel universes switch places, nobody notices. It's a common occurrence where I work. However, the particular parallel universe that the crew of the Enterprise switched with was evil.

So when Kirk returned to his quarters in the parallel universe and checked his service record, he found he had assumed command of the Enterprise by assassinating Captain Pike. Not a pleasant place, this parallel universe.

That episode was on my mind while I was shaving the other morning. It was staring me right in the face. There are tiny alternative universes right here on earth. Places where you can see yourself a little askew. Mirrors.

Mirrors have always been a source of mysticism. Vampires don't cast a reflection in a mirror. Break a mirror and you get seven years' bad luck. Alice fell through one. Kilgore Trout wrote they were leaks to other universes. Oddly, you are not the face you see in the mirror. You're seeing yourself backward, reversed; it's you but it's not.

While shaving, I noticed the mirrors in my bathroom were lined up to reflect off each other. In front of me was the face in the mirror and a mirror image of the face that looked into the mirror every morning. To really see myself as others see me, I needed a double reflection. An image even more distant than the face in the mirror.

And that's how we see ourselves. Askew. No matter how objective we are, we will never really know how we look to others because our vision is obscured by our own point of view. To really see ourselves as we are, we need to get as far as possible from our own self-perception.

In "Mirror, Mirror" the captain and crew get that far away, all the way to a separate universe. They view parts of their personalities that they strive to suppress. They are forced to see themselves as barbarians. And they can't deny that they are looking at themselves.

While going to a parallel universe isn't usually an option for most of us, stepping back and looking at ourselves is a good idea even with the distortion of self-perception. I suppose I relate to this episode because I wonder what it would be like to be a barbarian or a priest. How different would my life be in a different time and place? What would be different when I looked in the mirror?

My mind tends to wander, but being a small mind, it never wanders very far.

One of the differences between Star Trek and real life is that nobody ever daydreams on Star Trek. You know, just kind of stares off into space and thinks nothing. Kirk never has to tell Spock to wake up and smell the coffee. If I were Uhura, listening to that subspace radio chatter all the time, I'd zone out completely. She never does.

If I were Scotty down in the engine room with the drone of the warp drive going on and on, I would be daydreaming before you could say Jack Robinson. Not Scotty. Matter and antimatter, dilithium crystals, these things keep him endlessly focused.

Truth is, the truth this isn't. Long voyages make humans vegetate. Ask anyone who has ever taken a long car trip. Sing all the songs you want. Play all the car trip games in the world. After a little while, your mind will take its own little journey.

On a five-year voyage like the Enterprise's, I would probably daydream for a year and a half. I've refined these little trances into an art form. Coming out of a daydream, I can usually trace my thoughts backward until I reach the point where I drifted off. Try it if you like; I don't know if it's hard or easy to do, I just do it.

Ironically, many of my daydreams put me on the bridge of the Enterprise, the place where nobody daydreams. The fact that no one on the Enterprise daydreams probably isn't a conscious choice of the producers. My guess is it's a limitation of television drama.

While Star Trek is usually right on the big stuff, it does miss on some small points. This is one. Too bad. These little excursions are good for one's mental health.

Besides, on a show that takes place in outer space you'd think somebody would space out sometime.

Central to everything in Star Trek is the non-interference directive, the Prime Directive, as it is called. It may be the most important idea in the series. The way the directive is applied or not applied is as interesting as the concept of the directive itself. But let's not get ahead of ourselves.

The Prime Directive prohibits the captain and crew of the Enterprise from interfering in the internal affairs of any of the planets they visit. Say the Enterprise shows up at a planet where a human sacrifice is about to take place. They are prohibited from stopping the sacrifice.

Behind the Prime Directive is some pretty sound reasoning. People have the right to construct their societies in any way they wish. Valid reasons may exist why the sacrifice is taking place, reasons the crew of the Enterprise may not fully understand. Cultural bias may influence the way the crew interprets what they are seeing. Therefore it is best not to interfere in something you do not completely understand.

This rule not only protects the people of the planet, it protects the crew. Noninterference keeps the crew from getting into the middle of a private fight. Since they don't get involved, they don't have to pick sides.

Here's a different scenario. The Enterprise discovers a world that is being ravaged by a plague. Antibiotics on the ship could save the world. According to the Prime Directive, the Enterprise cannot interfere. Although they might save the inhabitants of the planet, they might also be put in the position of deciding who lives and who dies. Or, during the inoculation, advanced technology might fall into the wrong hands. Potentially, this advanced technology let loose on a backward world could produce results worse than the plague. Once again, the wisdom of the Prime Directive protects both the Enterprise and the life-forms it encounters.

If you understand the preceding, you should also understand this.

The Prime Directive is treated with as much respect as a fire hydrant at a dog show. Episode after episode after episode, Kirk ignores the Prime Directive and does what he believes is right.

Never doubt the captain would waltz right in and stop the human sacrifice. If the person to be sacrificed was an attractive young woman, never doubt the captain would fall in love. Next, he would pass out the antibiotics and end the plague. Kirk does observe the directive when it fits his purposes. Rarely otherwise.

In a way, the Prime Directive fulfills its primary mission: creating dramatic conflict.

What, then, is the lesson here? A great one. People are more important than rules. Enforce the spirit of the law above the letter of the law. The Prime Directive was instituted to protect people. When the directive gets in the way of protecting people, ignore it.

A person who understands a rule knows when to break it. A person who understands a rule understands intent. The Prime Directive was not intended to condone human sacrifice. Kirk does the right thing when he interprets the rule to fit the situation.

Wouldn't it be wonderful if our justice system could make that differentiation? We hate lawyers because they use the letter of the law to their own purposes. They pervert the spirit of the law. They make the right wrong, and the wrong right. Lawyers would let the human sacrifice take place, then sue on behalf of the relatives.

Watch virtually any episode of Star Trek and the Prime Directive will play a part. But Captain James T. Kirk will play a more important part. Judgment will be exercised. And people will be more important than rules.

Here's another reason James T. Kirk is an excellent manager. When he's around, you know he's in charge. When he's not around, he clearly designates his successor. It's simple and direct. Totally unmistakable. As he leaves the bridge, he turns to whomever he wishes to be in control and says, "Mr. Scott, you have the bridge." Mr. Scott then serves as captain while Captain Kirk is gone.

Anyone who has watched a teacher walk out of a classroom can appreciate the importance of this action. A smart teacher will appoint some skinny Goody-Two-shoes to spy on the class, someone who will tell on you in a minute. And guess what? It works.

A more absentminded teacher might mumble, "O.K. everybody work at your desk." Then leave. Guaranteed, immediate and total chaos will ensue.

But heck, why use grade school as an example? Let's talk about the average American office. While showing a little more restraint than the average grade school class—fewer spitballs will be thrown and fewer fist-fights will break out—from a productivity point of view, the profiles are similar. When the boss is away and no designate is around, less work gets done.

Like most of what Star Trek teaches us, this may seem simplistic. It is. These are lessons culled from a television show, not the library at Alexandria. But the lesson itself is right on the money.

Designate someone to take over the bridge, and the ship will continue to run smoothly. Designate someone to take responsibility for a job, and the job will get done.

In advertising, there is a job called proofreading. I'm sure you've heard of it. It's important because if you spell something incorrectly it reflects on what you are saying. "Give me liberty or give me depth" just doesn't have the same power as Patrick Henry's original quote.

Proofreading is not the occupation of choice for many people. For most, it's a way station. Proofread for a bit and get promoted to assistant copywriter. In smaller advertising agencies, there is no money for proofreaders. This is a constant trouble point.

At one small office I worked in, proofreading was everybody's job. True, our general manager believed that everyone who handled an ad should proofread it and everyone was responsible if an error got through. Needless to say, many errors got through. Why? Because when everyone is responsible, ultimately no one is responsible.

Big themes. The duality of man. Good and evil. Squeezing the toothpaste tube on the end or in the middle. Star Trek was different because it dealt with these issues head-on. To examine prejudice Frank Gorshin was painted half white and half black. Star Trek routinely tackled subjects other shows were frightened to touch.

A very early episode of Star Trek involved a transporter malfunction. Kirk was beamed back from a planet. As soon as he left the transporter room and the door shut behind him, the transporter came on again. Kirk materialized for a second time. But this Kirk was different—sinister.

Later we learn that the first Kirk is all good, the other is all bad. Somehow the transporter has scrambled the captain into two separate beings. Jekyll and Hyde, if you will.

And here's why Star Trek was a remarkable show. Instead of the usual battle between good and evil, a different point of view was drawn. Neither Captain Kirk was better than the other. Evil Kirk was a savage, practically a rapist, but he was strong-willed and determined. Good Kirk was very humane and caring but also timid, weak and lacking the ruthlessness to be a decision-maker.

Each Captain Kirk was incomplete without the other. Being completely good was just as bad as being completely evil. For the time and place, this was a tremendous breakthrough. And, as we say in advertising, it had the added advantage of being true.

Inside all of us is a killer and a priest. My mother used to say this in a beautifully simple way: "There's good and bad in everyone." What Star Trek made me understand is that everyone needs both the good and bad inside them to exist. It is finally a question of balance. For me. For you. For Kirk. For everyone.

Finnegan was an upperclassman at Starfleet Academy. An upperclassman who tormented a plebe he called "Jimmy me boy." Jimmy me boy was, of course, Cadet James T. Kirk. Long after Kirk graduated from the academy, the captain of the Enterprise remembered Finnegan.

"Remembered" isn't strong enough a word. What James Kirk wanted was to beat the tar out of Finnegan. And beat him silly he did—years later, on a planet that made dreams come true.

Virtually every member of the Enterprise lived out a fantasy on that planet, a planet constructed for the sole purpose of recreation. A planet constructed by an intelligence so far beyond our own, Spock wondered why they needed recreation at all.

The curator could have answered Spock. But it was Kirk who spoke. "The more complex the mind, the greater the need for the simplicity of play." Bingo. On the nose. Home run. Yeah, buddy. I'm gonna turn all the cards over. "The more complex the mind, the greater the need for the simplicity of play."

Other phrases may sound similar. All work and no play makes Jack a dull boy. Work hard and play hard. All those clichés are close but no cigar—they subtly miss the mark.

This is a prescription for maintaining one's mental health. An understanding that intelligence requires both purpose and diversion. That the more challenging uses a mind is put to, the more important it is to have fun. CEOs should scuba dive. CEOs must scuba dive. A vacation isn't just a good idea, it's an absolute need.

To tailor the concept a bit, the more complex the task (or job) the greater the need to build in some fun. Extrapolate this baby all over the lot. Star Trek strikes again. Everything you need to know is in this series someplace.

In this particular instance, it's also stated as eloquently as imaginable. The more complex the mind, the greater the need for the simplicity of play.

When I was a young boy in Catholic school, the nuns taught us the Golden Rule. Do unto others as you would have them do unto you. Good rule. You should treat other people as you would have them treat you.

Coming from the nuns, however, we considered this rule suspect. After all, the nuns frequently hit us. Strict interpretation of the Golden Rule would imply the nuns would like us to beat them up. We knew this to be false. Even raising your hand in self-defense when being struck by a nun could get you into big trouble. Principal's-office kind of trouble. Calling-your-parents kind of trouble. Never ever even think of hitting a nun—never. This was as clear as an unmuddied lake. Crystal clear.

While we struggled with this paradox, an offshoot of the Golden Rule puzzled us even more. The subrule was this: Treat everyone the same. Again, like the Golden Rule, not a bad sentiment. But in practice? Yikes! What a mess. Absolutely impossible to follow.

What was obvious to the students at Saint Joseph's School in Enfield, Connecticut, is not obvious to many current managers of people. You cannot treat everyone the same. Far from it. Managers with a feel for people know that you have to treat everyone differently. The rules should be fairly well spelled out, but how the people are treated inside those parameters should vary by individual.

For example, both McCoy and Spock work for Captain Kirk. Both are his friends. Both are experts beyond Kirk's abilities in their fields of specialization. Spock is a general scientist. McCoy is a medical doctor. Both are treated with respect and dignity. Mr. Spock, however, is allowed to override the captain's decisions. Kirk will in fact acknowledge Spock's abilities by turning to him for solutions and recommendations.

McCoy is usually told what to do. The captain's opinions are more important than McCoy's recommendations. Very often, Kirk will order McCoy to carry out a task against McCoy's protests.

One thing allows Kirk to treat these two so differently. He knows them. He understands their strengths and weaknesses. He wouldn't use Spock as a cheerleader or as director of human resources, and he knows that McCoy is a chronic complainer.

The creative department of an advertising agency isn't a starship, though there are some alien life-forms to be found there. But there are different fields of specialization, and many of the members of a creative department know much more about their fields of expertise than the creative director. You will also find emotionless people and chronic complainers. My guess is that this makes an advertising agency much like any other office.

To successfully manage all these different types of people, do what Captain Kirk did. Try to get to know them. All you can really manage is the strengths and weaknesses of your people. Then, when you know them and manage them in an individual way, try to do something else. Treat them as you would like to be treated.

All Star Treks end the same way. The captain is sitting in his chair on the bridge surrounded by the members of the crew. Significant others from the episode are sometimes part of the group. There on the bridge the moral of the story is told. Many times the moral comes in the form of a joke. A friend of mine calls this part of the show "the laugh on the bridge." As the laugh continues, the screen usually cuts to the outside of the ship. The epilogue music comes up and the episode ends.

Over time I came to realize that, more than a terrific way to end a television show, laughter is a great way to end almost any occasion. Nice way to end a business meeting. After a kiss, it's a great way to end a date. It would even be a great way to end the world. Imagine this, the Four Horsemen of the Apocalypse come galloping through, wreaking havoc on the world. Then, after a hard ride, they dismount, tell a joke, laugh, the music comes up, the universe goes down.

At work on some Fridays after four o'clock I like to gather the creative group together. Sometimes we sit in the computer area, other times we congregate in an office. The setting isn't as important as getting everybody together. Occasionally we send a writer out to the package store for a little beer. The purpose of these little get-togethers is part work, part social, part Star Trek. I figure if you can end the week with a laugh, it bodes well for the following week. When the sessions continue past five o'clock—quittin' time—I feel really good.

Endings are more important than beginnings. I hate that dandruff commercial that says, "You never get a second chance to make a first impression." The eventual outcome of a first meeting is far more important than initial impressions. Didn't the mother of the writer of that commercial ever tell him/her, "Don't judge a book by its cover"?

The first time Chuck Yeager flew in an airplane he got sick—sick. In World War II, Yeager made Ace in one day by shooting down five German planes during one mission. Chuck went on to become the first man to break the sound barrier. He led the first perfect deployment of a Tactical Air Command fighter unit squadron. Today General Chuck Yeager is generally considered to be the best pilot in the first one hundred years of aviation. Who cares if he threw up his first time in an airplane?

Most of the time you'll have a thousand second chances to make a good impression. First impressions can be overcome by a subsequent performance. But no one ever forgets how you go out. John Belushi, a funny man, is remembered as a drugged-out suicidal maniac. He can never live it down. Can anyone even remember their first impression of John Belushi?

And speaking of endings, there's always Lester Moore. Lester was shot to death in Tombstone, Arizona, in the wild 1870s. Not many folks know the story of Lester's life except that it ended when he met someone a little faster on the draw. He lies in Boot Hill Cemetery. At the head of his grave is a marker that reads:

HERE LIES
LESTER MOORE
FOUR SLUGS FROM A 44
NO LES
NO MORE

Now that's how to end an episode with a smile.

I **think it was Benjamin Franklin who said, "Guests, like fish, begin to stink after three days." Lovely thought there, Ben. To be fair, houseguests are both a joy and a pain. To be realistic, houseguests are going to happen. People will visit. The payoff for having houseguests is that you get to visit them and become their houseguest. But let's stay on the subject of people coming to visit you.**

How should one prepare for houseguests? Should one prepare for houseguests at all? Hey, they're coming to visit you. Why not show off in all your native charm? "This is our house. This is how we live. I'm sure you'll be happy just to fit in for the next few days."

It's an easy strategy for houseguests. Cuts down on a lot of the work. Just clean up the place and voilà, you're done.

I don't think so.

When guests are expected aboard the Enterprise, many modifications are made. Of course, many of the houseguests (shipguests?) aboard the Enterprise are aliens. Without some modifications in life-support systems, the visitors would die. And as any competent host will tell you, the death of your visitors is bad form.

The lesson here is straightforward. Change the environment of your home to accommodate your houseguests. Making your home more like their home will make them feel more comfortable and welcome. When your visitors are comfortable, they become better guests. How far you go is up to you. The idea is to make your visitors feel at home.

When my sister and her husband visit, I put a quilt on their bed. I normally leave the quilt in the closet, but my sister loves quilts and has one on her bed. Small changes like that can have large effects in making someone feel at ease. Besides, in my sister's case I know that soon after she arrives she will be in total control of the house. Why fight it?

O.K. Your houseguests have arrived and you've greeted them. Sit back and let everyone shake off the jet exhaust. Everybody settled? What's next?

Let's return to starship NCC 1701. Usually one of the first acts on the Enterprise after receiving guests is a formal dinner. Officers attend wearing their dress uniforms. The menu is top-drawer. Sometimes the food is from the visitors' planet, other times it is an earth favorite. Wherever the food comes from, it is made obvious, by a toast, that this feast is in honor of the visitors.

Feed the guests. Yeah, a great way to start a visit. Let's not take that part about the formal dinner too seriously. But a dinner in honor of your houseguests, with an appropriate toast, is a great place to start.

Next, ask yourself honestly, why did your guests come to visit? Did they come to see you? Did they come to see the city you live in? Is your home merely in a convenient locale? If you live in Orlando, you know the answer.

If they came to experience something other than your wonderful presence, take them out to eat. This is also good advice for bad cooks.

If your houseguests came to spend plenty of quality time with you, cook them dinner. Show them your silverware and wine collection. Do not treat your guests as guinea pigs. This is not the time to try out that oh-so-interesting recipe that you never had the opportunity to cook before. Play it safe. Serve a trusted standby that everyone loves. And don't forget the toast.

All right. You're off on the right foot. Is there anything else we can learn from Emily Post . . . ehh . . . Captain Kirk? Well, he usually assigns a crew member to give the visitors a tour of the ship, to be taken at their convenience, of course. Unless the guest is a beautiful woman, in which case he leads the tour personally. He also tries to keep everything as normal as possible during the visit.

If there is anything interesting around, at the very least give your houseguest the option of a tour. I live in Washington, D.C., about ten blocks from the White House. If a potential visitor gives enough warning, there is a VIP tour available that anyone can get just by asking. This is a big hit. You don't even have to go along.

As for the acting normal part, do what's normal for you. Be yourself. That's who they are visiting. I'm as much myself as possible (while following James T. Kirk's lead).

Great people talk about ideas. Average people talk about things. Small people talk about people. This is also the difference between television shows like Star Trek, a show about ideas, and shows like *Melrose Place,* which deal with who's zoomin' who. Star Trek episodes usually deal with themes like the dehumanization of man in a technological society. Typical prime-time fare deals with gossip.

It is truly amazing how much of our lives are filled with gossip. Titillating items about whatzisname and whatzername. If the time spent on gossip in the average office were added up, the loss of productivity noted would be in the billions.

Gossip is often confused with conversation. In fact, it often takes the place of conversation. Take gossip away from some folks and they would turn into mimes.

Bookstores and newsstands are gossip-crazy. Name your favorite type of gossip and there's a specialty magazine. Or ten. Entertainment, politics, finance, farming, pick a subject. We even create fake gossip like the *National Enquirer* because the factual gossip isn't enough for us. Give us dirty laundry. Why does anyone know who Marla Maples is? I mean really, who cares? Couldn't we live without that?

It becomes a game. Who knows what about who's doing

what to whom. The person who knows the most dirt has the most power. It doesn't even matter if the story is true, what matters is if it is juicy. And it matters if you're in. 'Cause if you're not in, you're out. Heaven forbid others might know more than you do. The game becomes self-perpetuating. Each turn of the screw deserves another. No matter who is getting screwed.

On Star Trek, the members of the crew don't gossip. There is plenty of opportunity for gossip, especially with Kirk's libido barely under control. But somehow the crew of the Enterprise figured out something that escapes a lot of folks—there are a heck of a lot more interesting things to talk about.

Ideas are one.

Kids walk into my office. Baby goats they are not. Young, aspiring advertising professionals. YAPs? They are well groomed, fresh faced, energetic. They carry books. Books in advertising are portfolios of previous work. The work of the young and fresh faced are spec ads. Spec ads are ads that have never been produced. Pretend ads. Virtually every portfolio, or book, has a spec ad for Crayola crayons and one for AIDS awareness. Usually the ads aren't very good.

I've scoured many episodes of Star Trek to see how young trainees are incorporated into the system. Can't really say I've found much help. Enterprise NCC 1701 is the flagship of the fleet. Very few cadets get the opportunity to join the crew. New members are more likely to be established professionals who require assimilation, not training.

The movies are a different matter. In *The Wrath of Khan*, the entire crew is trainees. Kirk is terrible with trainees. Maybe that's too strong. Kirk is not interested in trainees. Naturally, a situation develops in which the young trainees, under the watchful eye of the captain, must sink or swim. The training exercise is over, and now it's for real.

In one scene, Kirk turns to Spock and asks his opinion. How will this group of inexperienced trainees just out of Starfleet Academy perform? Spock answers, "Each according to his gifts."

Is this a cop-out? Sort of. It denies that you can teach someone a lesson that goes against his or her nature. Scared people will always be scared people. Brave people will react according to their gift of bravery. What is most important in life are the gifts you are given. If you are born with the gift of gab, maybe you can bore the Klingons to death.

Let us accept this premise, at least to a small degree. Kids can walk into my office day and night for years to come and what is important is the talent they are born with. The finest art schools in the nation can polish and polish them. But it won't help if they don't have the gift.

I just can't buy it. Here's why. Two things are important. For the sake of Spock, let us call the first one gifts. The second and more important factor is attitude, the willingness to overcome obstacles. To keep trying and never relenting. Persistence will overcome resistance.

By way of putting things into perspective, imagine a young fresh face walking into your office. Scrubbed clean. Eager. Feeling good about the meeting soon to unfold.

The absolute, number one, critical mistake this young person can make is this: acting like a jerk. You work hard. The folks in your office work hard. Weekdays often turn into weeknights. Weekends are often an extension of the work week. Pressure and stress are part of your daily routine. Now, ask yourself this question. Do you want to be around a jerk during a stressful sixty-hour work week? Do you want a nail driven into the bridge of your nose with a sledgehammer? Probably not.

Attitude is the top priority.

After attitude, talent or gifts are important. What Spock might have said was, "Each according to his desire and his gifts." But Star Trek got it half right.

So here it is. A young, eager, fresh-faced hopeful walks in the door. Find out what kind of a person is sitting across the desk. Is this someone you could spend long hours with? Is he or she positive?

Then find out about this person's gifts. In advertising, that means looking through their book for talent. Do they have a way of looking at products that is different from the pack? How do they think?

Kids walk into my office. Baby goats they are not. I've hired a few and they all have the same gift—a great attitude.

James T. Kirk has many attributes to be admired and emulated. He is loyal, helpful, friendly, courteous, kind, obedient, cheerful, thrifty, brave, clean and reverent. But make no mistake, Jim Kirk is no Boy Scout.

His greatest quality, one which I try to copy, is that he never gives up. He never quits.

Bones McCoy, standing on the Genesis planet, said it best. Above his head, the USS Enterprise was burning up in the sky like a streaking meteor. Next to him, James Kirk had just asked, "What have I done?" McCoy, eyes heavenward, replied, "You did what you had to do. What you always do. You took death and turned it into a chance to live."

So here's Kirk. His crew marooned, his son murdered, his ship destroyed, his reputation ruined, his career in tatters, his credit cards canceled. Not a good day for the boy from Iowa. What does the Captain do? He keeps his head. He figures out what to do next. He doesn't give up.

I've never faced the kind of adversity that Jim Kirk regularly defeats. However, I do run. Well, by many standards it's not running, but it is faster than jogging. The point is, I do go out dressed in running shorts and put one foot in front of the other.

During most runs, especially on hot days, the body wears down. Sometimes an ache will crop up to accent your tiredness. Slowing down or stopping pop into your mind.

When this happens during my runs, I think of James Kirk. It helps me keep going. Kirk wouldn't give up; he'd press himself harder, push through it and keep going.

This is not always the best advice. Once, during a 10K road race (that's 6.2 miles for the nonmetric of you), I really overheated. To gain seconds, I had skipped every water stop. The more tired I became, the harder I pushed. As I crossed the finish line, I collapsed. They threw me into the back of an ambulance and rushed me to a hospital.

As I awoke out of my delirium, the nurse asked if I could remember my name and address. This really upset me. What did she think, that I was an idiot? Then I realized I didn't know my name or address. I *was* a total idiot. Slowly it came back to me. My name was, still is, David Marinaccio. It took me a little longer to remember my address.

Neatly folded on my chest, next to the IV line, was a T-shirt. A race official noting that I had crossed the finish line gave me the T-shirt that was awarded to all the finishers.

Now, what I had done was extremely stupid. Never run a race without replenishing your fluids. It can kill you. But the part about never quitting, I'm proud of that. I was hot, tired and physically drained, and still I had summoned the strength and the willpower to run the entire distance. I didn't give up.

I still have that T-shirt. I believe it shows I have a little character. Not unlike my favorite character, a starship captain who never gives up.

To produce vodka in the United States of America, you must follow very restrictive rules. These rules require that the vodka be both odorless and tasteless. The rules work. In blind taste tests, American vodkas are indistinguishable from each other.

I learned this amazing piece of trivia in a conference room at an advertising agency in Chicago. This information was considered important because our job was to convince consumers that the vodka we were advertising was the best-tasting.

Our task was not impossible, though. You see, the very same consumers who could not distinguish a taste difference between vodkas in a blind taste test could find wide differences in taste when there were labels on the bottles. Since our bottle had a label on it, we were confident we could become the best-tasting vodka.

The researcher who told us these wondrous facts closed the meeting with a phrase that is an advertising mantra. She said, "Perception is reality." Her point was that we should treat these taste differences as if they were real.

To reinforce the perceived differences, we would create a "point of difference" from other brands of vodka. In our case, we would tell the public that our special filtering process is what produces the smooth, smooth taste you can find only in our bottles. Ironically, it is the filtering that makes all American vodkas absolutely tasteless. But hey, perception is reality.

In one episode of Star Trek, the Enterprise is grabbed by a giant hand. The ship cannot move forward or back, up or down. Engaging the ship's engines to pull free of the hand only results in the hand's squeezing harder.

The hand, of course, is an illusion. It is really an energy field made to look like a hand. By examining the hand, the Enterprise begins to unravel the mystery that is holding them motionless in space.

Unlike advertising agencies, the captain and crew of the Enterprise never accept perception as reality. If they did, they would still be in orbit trying to shake hands.

In "Spectre of the Gun," Kirk, Spock, McCoy and Chekov find themselves transported to Tombstone, Arizona, circa 1881. The entire town is an elaborate illusion. But the illusion is real enough to kill you—if you believe it can.

Once Mr. Spock realizes that the laws of physics don't operate in Tombstone, he concludes that the entire situation isn't real. He convinces the others of his discovery, and this becomes the key to resolving their predicament. What Spock does is find the reality behind the perception.

Perception is *not* reality. This is a running theme on Star Trek. Time and time again, situations that appear to be one thing are shown to be another.

It isn't necessary to watch Star Trek to learn this lesson. Think of the people you know. Some folks who appear cold and uncaring are often warm and decent when you get to know them. Smiling, friendly, outgoing folks can be downright mean when it counts. Image is shallow. What's important is the substance of a person.

Perception is perception. Reality is reality. Illusions must be examined to be exposed. But it is an effort well worth making. Because when you peel away the perception and find the reality underneath, you've also found the truth.

By the way, the vodka didn't sell and the brand went under.

Anyone with even a passing interest in Star Trek should know this rule: Never, ever, ever wear a red shirt—not under any circumstances. **Don't do it.**

Pick any episode. Captain Kirk, Mr. Spock, a series regular like Uhura and some guy you've never seen before are standing on the transporter pad. If the guy is wearing a red shirt, he will not live past the first commercial. Somewhere on the planet below certain death awaits.

I've watched these guys in red shirts get shot, be blown up, be disintegrated, have all their blood drained, have every cell in their body explode and otherwise meet the most painful and horrible deaths imaginable.

The endings aren't even especially heroic. First a guy beams down, then he's dead. At least it's usually quick. Nine times out of ten, the poor fellow doesn't have a clue what hit him. Within seconds, Bones examines the fallen crewman with a tricorder, turns to the captain and says, "He's dead, Jim." By the next scene it's as if the guy never existed.

There's no wake, no funeral and most of the time his name is never spoken again.

I bought red swim trunks once. Took them with me on a scuba diving trip to the Cayman Islands. While wearing those trunks ninety-five feet underwater on the north wall of the ten-thousand-foot-deep Cayman Trench, my regulator came apart. For those of you unfamiliar with scuba, the regulator is the thing you breathe with. No regulator, no air. Under ninety-five feet of water, this is more than an inconvenience. I managed my way up to the surface. Once safely back in my hotel room, I threw the red swimsuit away.

You would think I had learned my lesson. Wrong, security-detail breath. I bought a red short-sleeved shirt last summer. Next morning I unfolded the shirt and took out the pins. Ouch! A small trickle of blood. No big deal.

Work was relatively unremarkable that day, and I hopped into my car for the commute home. A car, I later realized, is a twentieth-century version of a transporter pad. On the ride home—WHAM. I ran into a van. My front end crumbled. The van sustained no damage.

Although I wasn't killed, there was several hundred dollars' damage to my car, and I did receive a $125 fine from the United States Park Police (one of Washington's many police forces). I tossed out the red shirt that night.

I do not own red socks or a red jacket or a red sweater or anything else that is completely red. It's a wonder I'm not afraid of Santa Claus. I do find red-haired women attractive but I don't recall ever dating one. That's probably for the best.

Listen, wear red if you want to, but I'll pass.

Whenever the captain and crew of the USS Enterprise visit other cultures, the customs of the host planet are observed. Alien societies are taken at face value and not judged by human standards. Even when Scotty's life hung in the balance in "Wolf in the Fold," his trial took place under the laws and penalties of Argelius II.

A friend of mine lived in a building on Peachtree Street in Atlanta. Of course, since every street in Atlanta is named Peachtree Street, that doesn't really tell you where he lived. His apartment was located in Midtown, an urban area of the city populated by numerous high-rises.

The particular building my friend called home was also the home of a large flock of pigeons. Like many of the residents of this building, my friend would occasionally feed the pigeons.

I've never really cared for pigeons—or air rats, as they are also called. Pigeons are dirty and always begging. They make a mess of any place they hang around. They even walk funny.

Let's face it, being a pigeon is no walk in the park. Worse still, they now face a fight for their ecological lives. Seagulls have swept into the cities to fight for their spot on the food chain. Even inland cities are now populated by gulls who find human trash and waste an absolute bonanza. They are bigger and faster than the pigeons, maybe smarter.

I don't have a shred of scientific proof to back up this observation, but it sure looks that way to me. Hey, I may not like pigeons, but I think they have a tough fight on their hands.

My friend recognized many of the pigeons that hung around his apartment building by their markings. One day he noticed that a bird he was familiar with had broken a wing. As the bird walked, he leaned to the side, his bent and ruffled wing dragging pathetically behind.

So heart-wrenching was the sight of this injured bird that he became an object of human pity. Passersby who saw him would break off pieces of their sandwiches for the poor little broken-winged bird. People would always make sure the aeronautically challenged pigeon got something to eat. He became a star. His weight ballooned. Surprisingly, his wing injury had become his lucky break.

Other pigeons noticed. No kidding, other pigeons noticed. Soon there was a rash of bogus broken wings. Perfectly healthy pigeons were pretending to have broken wings, hoping to gain charity from humans with food. And it worked. The faker birds got fed.

My friend had watched the whole phenomenon take place over the course of a week. He told me he didn't feed any of the others, but he continued to make sure the original broken-winged pigeon got his share. I sensed he didn't like the idea of the healthy birds pretending to be hurt. That they were fakers.

I think my friend is a smart guy. But I also think he fell prey to judging these pigeons by human standards. While feigning an injury to gain charity may be a reprehensible act for a human, the faker birds were just doing what had proven to be successful for another of their species.

We should treat pigeons like the crew treats alien species and keep our morality to ourselves. That applies to all animals and to nature in general. Fauna and flora have nothing to do with our culture. Following the lead of the crew of the Enterprise suggests giving respect and not passing judgment.

Hey, the pigeons were merely attempting to stay alive and prosper. In an environment where seagulls are now competing for the same space these birds occupy, they turned misfortune into fortune. Darn clever, too.

A starship captain is no different from a manager at K mart or IBM. One of the traits I admire most about James T. Kirk is the way he manages his people. I admire him as much for what he doesn't do as for what he does. Specifically, he doesn't use fear or threats as a management method.

A few years ago, there was a book called *Winning Through Intimidation*. It was a very popular book, although I don't believe it was too popular with the folks who were on the receiving end of the intimidation. I don't recall ever seeing a copy on the captain's bookshelf.

Scaring people may help achieve short-terms goals, but in the long run, it causes more harm than good. Loyalty, trust, respect—these are the qualities a good manager instills. They are incompatible with fear. And they can't be cultivated by a bully.

Though Kirk never resorts to fear, he is still a tough manager. Very tough. Captain Kirk regularly demands the impossible of his crew. He can demand it of them because he expects it of himself.

Kirk never asks them to do something he wouldn't do. When danger arises, he faces it personally. The safety of the crew of the Enterprise is his number-one priority. And they know it. So when the captain asks them to perform miracles, they do it.

In almost every episode of Star Trek, Kirk comes up with an array of superhuman demands. Scotty has to change the laws of physics to keep the warp drive going. He says he can't, but he manages to do it. Bones McCoy has to treat and save a creature without knowing its anatomy, or he has to cure a disease that no one has ever been infected by before. He always finds a way to get it done. The crew constantly surpasses their own capabilities because Kirk demands it.

Thing is, it works. I mean it works in the real world. Oh, you can't cure AIDS in an afternoon or discover a new scientific principle when you need one, but you can accomplish some amazing stuff if you *try* to achieve the impossible.

In advertising, the goals are modest compared to mixing matter and antimatter. The impossible might be changing a client's mind or finding the money to use a top-notch director to shoot your commercial or selling a particularly daring concept. Most times scaling these heights is not even attempted. Trying to conquer them in an atmosphere of bullying and intimidation is inane.

Fear is a powerful emotion. So is hate. One breeds the other. And when you are reaching, trying to go where no one has gone before, you better be sure that the people you're managing want you to succeed.

Great success is built on a solid foundation, a foundation of loyalty, trust and respect that you can depend on. Without them you will fail. With them you can command a starship.

The most touching thing about Star Trek is the friendship between Kirk and Spock. To me, it *is* Star Trek.

How and why friendships are formed is one of the great mysteries of the universe. Why do two people suddenly feel comfortable around each other? How do they find common ground? What is the connection that makes a relationship special, what gives it the strength to last?

Watching kids develop friendships is fascinating. Put two kids of approximately the same age together and BAM, they become as thick as thieves. A minute later they disappear. Just as you notice they're gone, they're back, laughing at a joke no one else understands. Kids seem to be able to do this an infinite number of times with an infinite number of other kids.

A few years later, this behavior is gone. It's not so easy for grown-ups. Maybe the reason adults don't make friends is that they have friends. I'm not sure. But somehow the process is different for big people.

There seem to be two basic kinds of friends. The peas-in-a-pod, birds-of-a-feather, friends-that-are-like-twins kind. Like Patty and Cathy, they look alike, they walk alike, at times they even talk alike.

Then there are friends like Kirk and Spock. Yin and yang, the opposite sides of the same circle, perfect complements to each other. Kirk needs Spock's coolness and calculation. Spock needs Kirk's gut instincts and aggressiveness. They complete each other.

I don't know when Kirk and Spock first met. I do know I've seen every single episode of Star Trek and every Star Trek movie but can't find that moment. Although we didn't get to watch this friendship start, we get to see it grow. We watch it being forged. Each adventure is a link in the chain. Every alien menace defeated is a shared victory. The more danger they share, the deeper the friendship becomes.

Countless times this pair risked their careers for each other. Kirk's travels up and down the chain of command are a testament to his devotion to Spock. Although he has killed the captain on at least two separate occasions, Spock is equally devoted to Kirk. The simplest way to put it is, they're friends for life.

Some friends merely save each other's lives. Kirk and Spock have died for each other. Kirk to save Spock in "Amok Time." Spock to save Kirk—the ship, too—in *The Wrath of Khan*. Now that's friendship.

Perhaps you know someone like that. Met in high school and never drifted apart. Moved away maybe, lived on different parts of the continent, but never lost that closeness. See him today and you just pick up where you left off. I'm lucky I have two friends like that.

Friends are one of the gifts of life. A funny thing about friends is that all the good times don't bring you as close as one shared bad time. Friends that go through hardships with you get to know you, and you them, in a deeper, more meaningful way. You get to see their best and worst. You see them for what they really are. In turn, they have seen you in exactly the same way.

Hit a rough spot, and a lot of people will help, if it's convenient for them. True friends will help even when they have to go out of their way. When you need them, they're there.

Often they're the same people who wouldn't dream of asking you for help when they need it. You still give it, of course, but the best of friends rarely need to ask anything of each other. Experience has taught me these things are true.

I know this: Kirk and Spock understand what friendship means. When I look at these two, I can't help but wonder what kind of friends William Shatner and Leonard Nimoy are. Can it all be acting? I hope not. I hope they're the best of friends for the rest of their lives.

Once when I was out of work, my brother-in-law invited me to play in a friendly game of poker. This poker game had taken place—off and on—over a number of years with pretty much the same players. Thousands of poker games just like it happen in dens and basements all over America. I was glad for the chance to get out, engage in some macho camaraderie and forget my current troubles.

As my financial situation wasn't the best at the moment, I was concerned about the stakes. "Quarter ante with a maximum fifty cents bump," my brother-in-law told me. For the uninitiated, that means it cost each player twenty-five cents at the beginning of each hand and that a player can raise the stakes fifty cents as each subsequent card is drawn.

"How much does the big loser usually lose?" I asked.

"About twenty dollars," he replied.

"O.K. Sounds good," I said, and gathered up twenty dollars in quarters for the night's competition.

As I met the other players I realized that macho camaraderie now includes females. Five men and a woman sat down to play cards.

Seven card stud was the game of choice. Two cards face down followed by five face up. I tossed in my quarter. After the first three cards were dealt, the bidding began. It hit fifty cents immediately. Same on the next card. Same on the next card. By the time the first hand ended, I had lost two dollars and seventy-five cents.

"Hey, what's the most anybody has ever lost in this game?" I asked the table.

"Harry lost about a hundred and twenty bucks," laughed the guy in the glasses directly across from me. I wasn't hungry, but I lost my appetite immediately. If looks could kill, my brother-in-law would have been dead.

My twenty bucks were gone in about five minutes. Players looked at me the way polar bears look at seals. Exchanging ten dollars for forty more quarters, I figured this was it. Lose 'em and I'm gone.

Then it came to me, the corbomite maneuver! A little trick James T. Kirk used to save the Enterprise. When you're outgunned and everybody knows it, it's time to bluff.

Kirk was in desperate straits. (At least it wasn't his brother-in-law that got him into it.) The Enterprise was facing an alien vessel far beyond its own technology. Ten minutes were given to the captain before he was to be blown to kingdom come. So Kirk, knowing his communications were tapped, sent a message to Starfleet. He said he would commit suicide by setting off the ship's supply of corbomite. The corbomite would destroy a large part of the galaxy, so the Federation shouldn't send any ships to this area for many years.

The aliens, who were eavesdropping, fell for the trick. And they retreated, leaving the Enterprise intact. Naturally, corbomite doesn't exist, even on Star Trek. Kirk was bluffing.

Next hand was my turn for the corbomite maneuver. Dealt

my usually crummy cards, I bet to the limit. Seeing this totally defeated figure—me—running up the pot was a clue to the other players. They quickly folded. I had bluffed and won a small pot. I had won. This little victory restored my confidence and I played the night, finishing slightly ahead.

I haven't played poker since. My sister's husband and I have made up. Thanks to the example of Captain Kirk, when strength failed, I successfully used guile. And like the captain, I learned that sometimes the greatest victory is just to escape with your skin.

Walter Koenig portrays Pavel Chekov, the Russian ensign, on Star Trek. I met him once, very briefly.

One day, a friend of mine who is also a big Star Trek fan was feeling sick. Being sick is bad enough, but it was also his birthday. Simultaneously, there was a Star Trek convention being held downtown. Putting two and two together, I hatched a plan. To cheer up my friend, I'd drop by the convention and buy him a phaser gun. Who wouldn't feel better holding a weapon that could kill or stun with the flip of a dial?

When I arrived at the downtown hotel where the convention was taking place, I discovered the price of admission was twenty-five dollars, exactly the amount of cash in my wallet. Entering the convention would be useless if I couldn't buy the phaser I came for. Disappointed, I headed for home.

Walking out to the lobby, I spotted a familiar face. Chekov! Standing next to him was a beautiful young woman.

(Not only the captain gets the girls.) They were saying good-bye, and Chekov, Walter Koenig, was heading toward the convention.

A new plan formed in my brain. I followed him, slowly closing the distance between us. To reach the rooms where the convention was being held, Chekov would have to ride down a long escalator. That ride would take about forty seconds, long enough for me to pitch my idea to the Star Trek cast member.

I stepped on the escalator a single step behind Chekov. Extending my hand and gesturing a handshake I said, "Walter, I'd like to thank you for many hours of enjoyment watching Star Trek."

He turned, took my hand, shook it and said, "Thank you."

"I wonder," I continued, "if you could help me with a small problem." Relaying the story about my sick friend and the lack of funds to accomplish my mission, I finished with a plea. "If you pretend I'm with you, I'm sure the ticket takers will just let us both pass into the convention free. It would be a big help."

Walter Koenig looked at me, paused a second, smiled, then said, "O.K." And we stepped off the escalator.

As we approached the convention doors, it was like being in a mini-tornado. Every head turned to see Chekov. The crowd at the door murmured. I could hear the voices: "It's Chekov." "Hey, look. Chekov." Almost everyone who saw him broke into a smile. It was a real, honest display of what people think about Star Trek, the happiness and magic of it. And because I was with Chekov, I got to taste a tiny little morsel of what it was like to be on the inside. It was wonderful.

Unfortunately, it ended as soon as we passed through the front doors. Walter Koenig turned to me and smiled a last time. "You're inside," he said. And he was gone, taking the little tornado of happiness with him.

Heading over to the merchandising area, I searched for a phaser. They were out. Instead I purchased a schematic diagram of the Starship Enterprise that cost about twenty dollars, leaving me cab fare home. As it turned out, it cost my sick friend about ninety dollars to have the gift framed. But hey, it's the thought that counts, right?

On the way home, I replayed those moments walking through the doors and into the convention with Chekov over and over again. I had gone to do something nice for a sick friend, or I would never have gotten to cross that threshold. And there's the lesson. When you do something nice for a sick friend, nice things come back to you.

Everyone is on the bridge of the Enterprise. Everyone. Kirk the white male, Uhura the black woman, Sulu the Asian, Chekov the enemy Russian, Spock the alien and guest stars of every gender, race and creed.

Best of all, on the Enterprise they all get along. More than get along, they all help each other. They're all part of the same team.

A quick look might make you think of the United Nations, but a longer look reveals what is really at work here, the melting pot. You don't hear as much about the melting pot these days. It's a beautiful concept. Immigrants from all over the world come to America and melt together. Each loses a little of their own culture but produces a brilliant alloy in which the best of each comes out.

The bridge of the Enterprise is the America of the melting

pot. O.K., there are no pointy-eared aliens from Vulcan in America. But it is a place where all kinds of people come together and become part of a greater whole.

It reminds me of the neighborhood of my youth. Walking around the block I grew up on, you could hear five different languages: Italian, French, Polish, Spanish and English. We all got along.

While many of the parents thought of themselves as Italian or Polish, all the kids thought of themselves as Americans. We loved baseball, rock bands, watching TV, the same stuff loved by American kids all across the country.

Today is different. Does that mean that for *The Next Generation* to realistically reflect America in the 1990s each ethnic group should be off in its own corner? That there should be gangs on the holodecks, drive-by shootings in the turbolifts and a McDonald's in Ten Forward? I hope not.

The truth is, the bridge of the Enterprise has always depicted a sanitized vision of America. But sanitized is not a dirty word. I see it as a hope for the future. If our country is going to live long and prosper, then we are going to have to behave like Kirk, Uhura, Sulu, Chekov and Spock. We don't have to dress in silly little uniforms. But we will have to give up a little of our pasts to share a common future. To gain the best of each other.

When my grandfather passed through Ellis Island in 1895, he came to the melting pot. He wanted to be part of America. His future and America's future were more important to him than where he came from. In America, it didn't matter where you came from. It mattered where you were going.

It's exactly the same on the bridge of the Enterprise. What is important is what you can contribute, not whether you came from Russia or Vulcan. The crew members must give up a little of themselves, but they gain the universe.

Star Trek: The Next Generation. I remember the first time I heard the phrase. The idea that there would be a Star Trek without Kirk, Spock and Bones seemed sacrilegious. Still, when the series began, I watched.

Mostly I didn't like what I saw. Captain Picard was too cold. Commander Data was such an obvious attempt to re-create Spock it seemed absurd. Nothing seemed right. Still, I watched.

Wesley Crusher became a member of the bridge crew. A child as a navigator? These guys were totally losing it. Still, I watched.

I was reminded of the last films of the Marx Brothers. Groucho was slower and the stories were thinner. Still, slow, thin Marx Brother movies were better than no Marx Brothers movies. And so it was with *The Next Generation*. At least it was Star Trek.

Slowly, things began to change. *The Next Generation* started to grow on me about the time Lieutenant Worf's hair started to grow on him. During the first couple of seasons, Worf wore his hair in a pageboy. Imagine, a Klingon in a pageboy. A member of the most vicious, warlike species in the galaxy, and these guys had given him a haircut that be-longed on Sandra Dee. It could have been worse. He could have had a beehive. To give it the real Klingon touch, they could have added real bees. Anyway, when Worf's hair began to grow, they were finally starting to get it—to understand Star Trek. They realized Worf was a Klingon and that warriors don't get their hair done by Sassoon.

Although the show was gaining steam, there were still some problems. Without a doubt, the worst was Deanna Troi's uniform. Deanna Troi, the ship's counselor, wore a special boob uniform. A deep V-cut revealed her ample cleavage. The fact that she was the only person on the ship to wear a boob uniform ran counter to the best notions of Star Trek.

Star Trek is not about cheap sex. Star Trek was out in front—perhaps the wrong expression—in understanding that women are the equals of men and in portraying them as equals. The boob uniform was thought up by, well, boobs. I haven't noticed the boob uniform in a while. I hope it's gone forever.

Somebody finally wised up and sent Wesley Crusher off to Starfleet Academy. Don't get me wrong, Wil Wheaton does a great job as Wesley. It's just that Picard was right in the first place. Children don't belong on the bridge.

Ultimately, the optimistic outlook of the original Star Trek found redemption in *The Next Generation*. It got better and better. Intriguing concepts began to take shape. Species that communicated through analogy and the dreams of an android were explored. The classics were woven into the scripts.

On the original series, Shakespeare was often a part of the show. A passing theatrical troupe performs Hamlet during "The Conscience of the King." The three witches from Macbeth make a cameo appearance in "Catspaw." The Star Trek movies are practically homages to the Bard. In *Wrath of Khan*, Ricardo Montalban's death scene is pure Shakespeare. *Star Trek VI: The Undiscovered Country* draws so heavily on Hamlet, I was expecting Mel Gibson to show up.

The Next Generation won me over completely and totally when my literary hero, Mark Twain, showed up at his acidic best, gracing the final cliff-hanging episode of one season. I wish Hal Holbrook had been playing the part, but you can't have everything. Besides, it was a very good Sam Clemens who matched wits with and then joined the crew of the Enterprise D.

In my heart I wanted *The Next Generation* to succeed. It just took me a while to warm up. Given time, *The Next Generation* was able to connect with my generation. Often we (meaning me) are a little quick to judge, quick to condemn. I'm glad I kept watching. Good things are worth waiting for.

If there's a lesson to be learned here, it is about the real next generation. With kids, a little patience is a good idea, too. Children will usually surprise you with how well they turn out, it just takes 'em a bit of time.

What will people do in the twenty-third century? What are the occupations of the future? Hmmm? The military will be intact. Hence, captains, navigators, chief engineers, communication specialists, yeomen and gunners will all be around. Doctors and colonists are a good bet. Bureaucrats are indestructible. Bartenders are indispensable. And chaplains will always be in demand.

Star Trek has a place for them all. They've all played parts in one episode or another.

But dare we dream that the future will be minus one occupation? That the future will be free of lawyers?

Alas, lawyers continue to exist into the twenty-third century. Hey, Star Trek presents an optimistic view of the future, not a perfect one. Kirk was defended by a member of the bar when he went on trial for murder in an episode called "Court Martial."

The kindly lawyer that took Kirk's case was right out of a 1930s movie. His sense of the law as an instrument of justice was refreshing by today's standards. Even the prosecutor, a former girlfriend of Captain Kirk, was that uncommon breed of lawyer that cared about justice and people. She was happy to lose the case when it was discovered that Kirk was innocent.

Amazingly, money never came up during the entire episode. Imagine two lawyers and neither interested in money. Cynics could use that as the ultimate proof that Star Trek is fantasy.

I, however, choose to believe that in the future even lawyers will join the human race. That the law as a profession will end its obsession with money and refocus on the higher meanings of the law.

I offer as proof the simple observation that no one has ever filed suit against Captain Kirk. If members of the bar were to continue their current behavior into the future, surely someone would have tried to sue the captain. Lord knows he's punched enough people to spend the rest of his natural days in litigation.

Ipso facto the future is a place where tort reform has turned lawyers into wholesome, functioning members of society. Instead of suing everyone in sight, people will actually solve their problems outside of courtrooms. Lawyers will still exist to handle the criminal proceedings of the day, but their primary concern will be finding the truth, not joining the million-dollar-settlement club.

The future according to Star Trek has puppets, paupers, pirates, poets, pawns and kings. It even has room for lawyers. But mercifully, the ambulance chaser has disappeared into history. Hooray!

James T. Kirk and all members of the crew of the Starship Enterprise are sworn to obey the orders of their senior officers. This is the military code of conduct. Survival of the chain of command rests on strict adherence to it. Disobedience cannot be tolerated. It would invite a complete breakdown of order.

For this reason, it is surprising that one of the strongest suggestions of Star Trek is to question authority. Look at virtually any authoritarian society the Enterprise visits. They're usually a disaster. Check it out.

On Gamma Trianguli VI the followers of Vaal had turned into a race of sheep until Kirk ordered phasers to knock out Vaal's power source.

Countless generations of Yonadans had lived in ignorance and servitude under the strict discipline of the Oracle until Kirk used phasers to knock out the Oracle's power source.

Near Pollux IV, the entire crew of the Enterprise was almost enslaved under the iron hand of Apollo until Kirk used phasers to knock out Apollo's power source.

. . . Wait a minute, I just had déjà vu. Sorry. Where were we? Oh yeah.

And speaking of authoritarian societies, let's not forget about Professor Gill. He reinstituted Nazism—with the best intentions, of course—on Ekos. This civics experiment failed miserably until Kirk woke the führer out of a drug-induced semicoma.

I believe I can see a pattern here. Absolute power, which is what Vaal, the Oracle, Apollo and Gill had in common, corrupts absolutely.

Authority was seen as anathema to original and independent thought. Kirk's goal was to get the residents of these societies thinking for themselves, to get people of these planets to stand on their own two (or however many) feet. Phaser fire usually got the oppressed citizenry on the road to their full potential.

When Star Trek first appeared, everyone was challenging the status quo. Cultural, sexual and civil rights revolutions were in high gear. People were marching in the streets because they believed the United States government had lost its way. "Down with the establishment" and more offensive idioms were a part of everyday speech. But I do not believe Star Trek's perspective was some ephemeral view of life dictated by the 1960s.

In fact, the most monumental confrontation with authority by Captain James T. Kirk didn't occur until the late 1980s. *Star Trek V: The Final Frontier* climaxed in a confrontation between Kirk and God.

God tells Kirk to bring the Enterprise closer to the planet that the captain, Bones and Spock have beamed down on. Kirk doesn't comply. Instead he asks, "What does God need with a spaceship?" Bones interrupts, "You don't question the Almighty." But Kirk ignores the doctor and asks again. Captain James Tiberius Kirk not only questions authority, he questions God.

As it turns out, the entity the captain was talking to was not God. Powerful, yes, but not God. For, as any good captain knows, God doesn't need a starship.

If Kirk had submitted to the apparent deity, if he hadn't

questioned, the outcome would have been terrible. Kirk's insolence saved the galaxy.

Well, it wasn't actually the captain's questioning that saved the galaxy. You might suspect that it was Kirk using phasers to destroy the entity's power source. But in this case, it was Mr. Spock using a Klingon disrupter to destroy the entity himself. Hey, that's what you get for impersonating God.

Technology changes, but people don't. No matter how powerful our computers become or how many diseases we learn to cure, we still act dopey.

Take cars. I can't say that Star Trek definitively implies there are cars in the future but whenever they show San Francisco in the Star Trek movies, there are carlike things flying around. For the sake of convenience, let's just call 'em flying, nonpolluting, technologically advanced vehicles of the future. Wanna bet that some dopey human will lock his keys inside? I'll give you odds. No matter how advanced the car, we will lock our keys inside, forget to set the parking brake or smash into the flying, nonpolluting, technologically advanced vehicle right in front of us while we are changing the radio station. Because, while the cars may change, the humans driving them remain the same. It's our lot.

Have you ever watched the fire-fighting competitions on television? Firemen from all over America compete in events like the ladder climb or the hose hookup. Obviously, these are the best, most physically fit firemen from their towns. Ever wonder who is left behind in the fire station to protect the citizenry? I'm just waiting for a town to burn down while its firefighters win the competition as the nation's best. It's just dumb enough to happen.

I read once that a hunter shot a cow because he mistook it for a squirrel. This is our species I'm talking about.

Star Trek does acknowledge this klutzy side of humanity. In "A Piece of the Action," the first thing Kirk does after starting up an antique automobile is to take off in reverse. A finicky computer in "Tomorrow Is Yesterday" insists on calling him "Captain, dear." And he sits on a furry little animal occupying his chair in "The Trouble with Tribbles." Hardly high comedy but very human.

Yeah, I know, Captain Kirk never overdraws his checkbook or burns the roof of his mouth on any of the shows. But if we watched his whole life, I'm sure we'd find something as dopey as my performance in a restaurant not long ago.

Out to dinner with friends and sitting across the table from my date, I noticed something scary. She seemed to be choking. I shot out of my chair but was unable to get to the other side of the table. I started to panic. Shouting as loudly as I could, I called out to the others, "Lamaze, Lamaze, someone give her Lamaze." The table broke out in laughter. My date recovered and smiled. She was fine; she didn't need the Heimlich maneuver and she certainly didn't need Lamaze.

I believe I would fit in fine in the twenty-third century.

Political correctness is a hot topic these days, although I'm not really sure what it means. Politics is one of the least respected professions around the world. The idea that anything associated with politics could be correct seems incorrect to me. It's like

George Carlin's mutually-exclusive-words routine. Certain words just do not go together. Comedian Carlin used examples like *jumbo shrimp* and *military intelligence.* Let me add *political correctness* to the list.

There are words that do belong with *political. Expedience*, for example, *political expedience.* See how nicely they fit together. *Political tricks* and *political patronage* have a ring. *Political suicide.* A good idea, but probably a little too much to hope for. And then there's the place where all politicians belong, the *political asylum.*

While I admit I'm suspicious of anything politically oriented, there was one political correction I highly approved of. Star Trek changed its mission statement. In the old days, Captain Kirk said, "These are the voyages of the Starship Enterprise. Her five-year mission: to explore strange new worlds, to seek out new life and new civilizations, to boldly go where no man has gone before."

Today, Captain Jean-Luc Picard says, "These are the voyages of the Starship Enterprise, its continuing mission to explore strange new worlds, to seek out new life and new civilizations. To boldly go where no **one** has gone before."

The change is subtle and meaningful. It's not the in-your-face politics of division. It's simply the acknowledgment of a fact. Women have played and will play an important role in the exploration and discoveries of space.

By changing "man" to "one," Star Trek addressed an old error. Now the mission statement is definitely correct. There's really nothing political about it.

What is it about Star Trek that inspires the people who watch it to be so . . . inspired? My whole life I've run across people who draw parallels between their existence and the fictional characters aboard the Enterprise. I'm not talking Trekkers or fanatics. Just folks like you and me who make reference to Star Trek at work, at home and at play. What makes this short-lived television series of the 1960s so powerful?

Initially, the actors who portrayed the captain and crew had no clue. William Shatner said in an interview, "We were just actors, performing on a weekly TV series."

No, you weren't, Bill. You were touching people in a way they had never been touched before. You were transporting audiences to a place they never wanted to leave. And once you took us there, we never let you go back either.

I remember the first time I watched Star Trek. My mother and my brother Mark were there. Small bowls of Neapolitan ice cream sat in our laps. Before the episode ended, Star Trek was my favorite show. I couldn't wait for next week or to tell my friends about the show.

In high school, we often discussed episodes of Star Trek with a fervor never applied to our studies. I remember sitting in my friend Jim's Ford Fairlane talking about "Who Mourns for Adonais?" an episode that postulates that the ancient

Greek gods were really space travelers. Thousands of years later, the Enterprise stumbles upon the remnants of this group on a planet far from earth. Apollo is the lone survivor.

The discussion made us giddy. We talked and laughed and played with the idea. It was as if the Enterprise's warp drive had been put directly on our imaginations. We thought thoughts as big as the galaxy.

There were undoubtedly a thousand similar discussions taking place all across America. And with syndication, the same discussions were probably taking place all across the globe. Were two German high schoolers sitting in a Volkswagen having the same exchange? Two Swedes in a Saab? Two Italians in a Fiat? Why not? If the Greek gods were space travelers, anything was possible.

In a way, Star Trek made us all one, the people of the planet earth. We had a common vision. And in 1968, for the first time in history, NASA astronauts took photographs of the whole planet from space. So we got to see what our vision really looked like. Maybe that's it. That Star Trek and the times and science all came together at one moment. That we suddenly looked at ourselves in a whole new way. And that once we saw that perspective, we just kept it. Maybe that's why so many people still do it today.

Then again, maybe the ability of Star Trek to touch us is a mystery of the universe. If so, then just letting it inspire us is more than enough.

Lieutenant Commander Montgomery Scott is the perfect ship's engineer. His love for propulsion systems know no bounds. Given shore leave, he would rather go back to his quarters and read technical manuals. All the better to understand the most technologically advanced vessel of his time, his vessel, the Enterprise.

Scotty treats this piece of machinery as if it were a person. He coaxes it, he pushes it, at times he is more wet nurse than chief engineer.

The ultimate goal of all this loving care is speed. If the ship's maximum speed is warp seven, then he just knows he can edge it up to warp nine. And maybe just a wee bit more.

He lives in a tug-of-war. One side loves the ship, wants to treat it like a baby. The other side tortures the ship until the last ounce of speed is squeezed out of the warp drive. And then he squeezes just a wee bit more.

Scotty loves to break the rules. If he has a theory that's never been tried before, then the Enterprise is a guinea pig for his idea. Never satisfied with the status quo, he tinkers and changes and improves, making up the manual as he goes along.

The lesson I learned from Scotty is to leave all the options open. When dealing with complex problems, humans want to simplify them, idiot-proof them. We live in a society where everything is idiot-proof. By the way, you and I are the idiots things are idiot-proofed for.

There is a slight problem with living this way. Idiot-proofing is also genius-proofing. Idiot-proofing reduces the impact of judgment. On the Enterprise, all the rules can be broken if there is a good reason. Greatness is usually achieved by trying something different or putting existing things together in new and unconventional ways. It's called innovation. Idiot-proofing prevents new approaches, ensuring that the same old tried and true methods are used.

Scotty's genius could not find expression in an engine room with a governor on the warp drive. Idiot-proofing the Enterprise would mean limiting the chief engineer's creativity. Idiot-proofing would mean more rules to follow and fewer options to be exercised. With fewer options, it's safe to say, the ship would have blown up long ago.

Competent people know which rules to follow and which to ignore. When people of good judgment are allowed to exercise their insights, good results usually follow. When people's hands are tied, they are ineffective.

The crucial variable here is competence. Sure, if a bunch of trainees are running the ship, idiot-proofing is probably called for. But when you're working with the best, let 'em loose. Don't restrict them. And you, just like Captain Kirk, will be the beneficiaries of their genius.

Doctor Leonard McCoy is the perfect ship's physician. Just kidding. The character created by DeForest Kelley is cantankerous, contrary and opinionated. Underneath, of course, he has a good and caring heart. Bones McCoy's view of the world is just a bit cynical.

His cynicism usually serves him well. He sees right through Mr. Spock. He can tell off the captain if he has to. And you'll never find him backing down an inch from something he believes in.

Cynicism also gives him a gift that is useful in any age. It allows him to use technology without being subservient to it. The tools of medicine in the twenty-third century are highly sophisticated. There are the tricorder, the medical scanner, the sterile field and various computers. There are also highly complex vaccines and compounds for almost any situation.

These tools are useful to the doctor. But McCoy understands that they are only tools. When these devices fail to work or start to hinder rather than help the process, McCoy changes the way he works. He uses his years as a doctor, his judgment and his creativity to find solutions. In short, Dr. Bones McCoy knows when to shift from high-tech to low-tech.

In "The Devil in the Dark," Kirk wounds an alien creature

called a Horta. A mind-meld between Spock and the Horta confirms that the Horta is injured very badly. The mind-meld also reveals the intelligent nature of the alien. Kirk orders McCoy to heal the Horta. Unfortunately, the Horta is a silicon-based life-form. Its body structure is more mineral than animal. The creature is a living rock.

At first McCoy hesitates. "I'm a doctor, not a bricklayer," he protests. But he examines the creature. The good doctor's instruments are designed for examining human beings and prove ineffective. What follows is—in my humble opinion—McCoy's finest moment.

He puts down his tricorder and orders emergency shelter cement from the Enterprise. Emergency shelter cement is mostly silicon. So, he trowels the cement into the Horta's wound as a bandage. Sure, it means getting his hands dirty, but it works!

"I'm beginning to believe I could cure a rainy day," McCoy tells the captain. And I believe he's right.

In advertising, we use computers. In the past decade they have become the tool of choice for many art directors and designers. The computers can perform extremely quickly. Representations of print ads can swiftly be brought to near-finished quality by using any number of programs. These "comp" representations help clients see what their ads will look like in a magazine or newspaper.

This tool is a wonderful advance for our business. However, it is sometimes quicker to draw a picture or to insert an exclamation point by hand. And there are some things the computer just cannot do. Low-tech occasionally has advantages over high-tech.

When these instances occur, many art directors get stuck and forget there is a world outside the computer, a world filled with pads and X-Acto knives and magic markers. Many times these low-tech tools in the real world can do the job better and faster than a one-gigabyte hard drive. Oh, they may get your hands a little bit dirty, but you'll get the job done.

An art director who gets the job done is valuable—more valuable than one with clean hands. The same applies to anyone in an occupation that mixes new technology with more traditional implements. The best employees are the ones who use all the available resources, especially their judgment.

As Doctor Leonard "Bones" McCoy showed us, kneeling over that Horta, technology is a tool, but it's not the only tool. And there are times when it's the wrong tool. Thanks, Doc.

Advertising agencies are always bragging about what great listeners they are. They'll tell anyone who'll listen.

I think what they are really trying to tell their clients is that they can communicate with them. That they understand them. Instead, they just say they listen. Taken literally, that means they do only half the job. After all, communication isn't just listening, it's exchange.

Listening is a big industry. There are books, tapes, videos and seminars on listening. I've sat through many talks given by people who were experts on listening.

No doubt listening is an important skill. But to have a meaningful dialogue, listening isn't enough. I mean, you can't have two people sitting there listening to each other and accomplish anything. On the other ear, one person doing all the listening and another doing all the talking isn't productive either.

"Language, you depend on it for so much, but is anyone its master?" So spoke Mr. Spock in "Is There in Truth No Beauty?" Well, sort of. Mr. Spock had mind-melded with Kolos, the Medusan ambassador, when the statement was made. Judging by the wide grin on Spock's face when he spoke, the observation likely came from the ambassador, who was rattlin' around in the first officer's brain.

The short answer to the ambassador's question is "No." A solid case can be made that far from mastering language, no one even uses it adequately.

I recall learning in my child development classes to go beyond speech when interacting with children. Small children can't always find the right words to express themselves. Many times they don't even know the right words. The idea is to listen to what kids are trying to communicate instead of listening to what they are saying.

Preschool is as wild as any planet the Enterprise ever visited. Man-eating four-year-olds regularly snack on their playmates. Power plays and shifting alliances create a maze seasoned politicians would have trouble negotiating. Love buds, blooms and dies in the afternoon. And virtually all of it is nonverbal. Noisy, but nonverbal.

I mention this because in subsequent years I've become convinced that preschoolers communicate as well as adults (possibly as well as worldwide communication companies). Their exchanges are brief, to the point, and for the most part honest.

Still, economy with words isn't the answer to mastering language either.

I had an uncle who never finished a sentence. He'd kind of trail off about halfway through a thought and leave it hanging there. Then he'd start the next sentence. Drove me crazy. Even weirder was the fact that we all understood him. Somehow we all knew how the sentence would end, so he never had to conclude. Besides, in my family someone was always interrupting. So, none of us ever finished a . . .

I believe if the Medusan ambassador had shared Mr. Spock's body for a little longer he could have answered his own question. He would have understood that language is only part of communication, just as listening is only part of language. Subtle movements and actions help us interpret words. Sometimes no words are needed at all. Like a nursery school teacher, Kolos would have learned that what was being communicated is more important than what is being said. Or heard.

And understanding that, he could have had real exchange with humans. With luck, he might even have been able to decipher what a multinational advertising agency meant when it talked about listening.

You meet an unusual assortment of traveling companions on a bus. I'm not talking about going a couple of blocks in the city, although you can meet interesting people on a city bus, too. I'm talking about the kind of bus that crosses state lines.

Given the duration of that type of trip, an eight-by-forty-foot box is just too cramped to maintain any hope of personal privacy. So even though elbows, perfumes and conversations invade your personal space, it just makes good sense to go with the flow and try to be friendly. A smile or kind word can help the hours pass a little more easily. You're all in it together. Make the best of it.

Some folks hunker down in their seats and bury themselves in books. Others love to chatter away. I have a slight fault. When people talk loudly, I tend to look at them. Once eye contact is established, the talker will usually lock in on me. This makes me uneasy, so I say something. Soon, I'm in a conversation—like it or not.

So it came to be that a bantamweight boxer, an unemployed roofer with a large protuberance that ran from his nose to his forehead and I were sitting in the back of a bus headed out of New York City.

The boxer carried much of the early conversation. He also carried a bottle of cheap whiskey in his pocket. In short order he knocked off the whiskey, which in turn knocked him out.

The roofer and I had stories to exchange. I had worked my way through college as a roofer and appreciated how hard the gentleman next to me worked for his money.

As we talked, the roofer said something unbelievable. "I can drive an eightpenny nail into a two-by-four with my head."

"What?" I wittily replied.

He grinned and asked me to touch his forehead. Now, I had noticed the large bulge in his forehead, but I hadn't mentioned it. Hey, if you sit down next to a guy with a large bulge in his forehead, discretion is usually the best course to follow.

"Go ahead, touch it," he insisted. So I did. I felt as if I were touching a Klingon. Luckily, this was a very friendly Klingon.

I asked, "Can you really drive an eightpenny nail into a two-by-four with that?"

"Yeah, won a lot of money on bets doin' it." He paused. "It's hell to pay if I miss."

That cracked me up. I mean, you know that's got to be the truth. Of course if he did miss, he would lobotomize himself at the same time he lost the bet. So he probably wouldn't care much about losing the money.

We woke up the boxer when we hit Hartford. And each of

us went our own way. Without the bus, we would have never touched each other's lives. Like I said, on a bus you meet a strange assortment of people.

There are folks just like the boxer and roofer on Star Trek. One is Harcourt Fenton Mudd. Another is Cyrano Jones. Both travel through space in small spaceships living lives we can hardly imagine. Jones buys and sells rare and useless merchandise, while Mudd, the con man, peddles dreams.

Mudd and Jones live in the margins. The Enterprise encounters them only by coincidence, when their courses collide. They're a part of the same universe as the Enterprise, but they don't fit in the perfectly ordered world of a starship.

Jones and Mudd are a reminder of the same lesson I learned on the bus ride. Many lives have little to do with the nine-to-five world that the rest of us have made for ourselves. The variety of ways to pass through this life are endless. We think of ourselves as normal, but who's to say?

Right now, there's a guy out there driving eightpenny nails into two-by-fours with his head. I hope he doesn't miss.

Making a telephone call is a simple act. I don't mean to say it is easy. It can be one of the most difficult acts for a human to perform. I remember my sophomore year in high school. Sitting alone looking at the telephone, I would summon all the nerve in my fifteen-year-old body. This great effort would occasionally result in my being able to pick up the receiver. But I couldn't seem to dial.

If I could have dialed, the number my digits fingered would have connected me to the home of Beth K. I desperately wanted to talk to Beth. To ask her on a date. But my fear was overwhelming. What if she didn't like me? What if she rejected my advances? The closer I came to the phone, the greater my anxiety would become. I gave in to fear. I never called.

Over time I realized that if you can dial a telephone, you can do anything. That simple action is all that is necessary to launch almost any human endeavor.

You want to skydive? Call a skydiving club. Had an argument with a close friend you want to settle? Call 'im. Want to find a preschool for your kid? Call. Half the time there's an 800 number to get you started. Just pick up the phone and dial.

I am aware that people don't actually dial the phone anymore. Although button-pushing is the action required to make a telephone work today, I still think of it as dialing. Of course, I still think of time in quarters. Quarter of one, quarter past seven—those phrases seem more natural than twelve forty-five or seven-fifteen. When I look at digital clocks and push-button phones, I remember when the world was rounder. Anyhow, just grab the cordless and punch in the numbers, and the world can be yours.

It's the first step to anywhere. It turns thought into action. Dreams into reality.

Hey, Star Trek began with a call—a distress call that led the Enterprise to Talos IV. Starfleet calls are often the stimulus for an episode. Apollo took AT&T's advice literally and reached out and touched the Enterprise. That started a wonderful adventure.

But I'm sure there was an important Star Trek phone call made before any of those—the call to Gene Roddenberry from NBC telling him they had bought his TV show.

Over time, even teenage angst can be turned into wisdom. I'll never know what would have happened if I made that call to Beth K., what adventures might have been. In subsequent years I've learned to pick up the telephone and dial. The result hasn't always been what I wanted, but it sure beat sitting there looking at the darn thing. Give it a try. Pick up the phone and see what happens. It's far better to act than to wonder what might have been.

Take one second. One hundred seconds is about a minute and a half. One thousand seconds is about seventeen minutes. A million seconds? One million seconds will take twelve days to pass. Now guess how long one billion seconds is? Take a second to figure it out. Take a hundred seconds and do the math. The answer will take your breath away.

One billion seconds is over thirty-two years—years. It's a big number. It looks like this: 1,000,000,000.

As large as that number is, it is dwarfed by the number of stars in our galaxy. The Milky Way contains approximately one hundred and fifty billion stars. 150,000,000,000 looks like that.

With so many stars out there, it begs a question: Why haven't we discovered a single intelligent species in our galaxy besides ourselves? Why isn't there an artifact or radio wave or signal that positively indicates life beyond the earth? Why isn't there a single shred of proof of the existence of an alien race?

Forget intelligent races, we haven't even proved there is a space fungus or alien microorganism. For all our science and discoveries, we are the only living things in a dead universe.

I am aware of the abduction phenomenon, claims that

people have been captured and experimented on by aliens, then returned to their homes. I've seen the "In Search Of" episode on the Roswell, New Mexico, alien crash site. I've actually met people—nice, credible people—who have had UFO experiences. But these people and events have not produced a piece of absolute, undeniable scientific proof.

I, however, believe the Milky Way is teeming with life. It must be. Otherwise how could Kirk, Spock and McCoy stumble upon inhabited planet after inhabited planet? Hey, nearly every week a new alien life-form is introduced on Star Trek. Ergo, we live in a galaxy filled with an array of beings, sentient and not.

Many scientists believe right along with me. The United States government funds a project called SETI (the Search for Extra-Terrestrial Intelligence). Actually, it *used* to be called SETI. The new name for the project is the High Resolution Microwave Survey. Brave congressmen worried that the name SETI, which contains the letters ET, might prove an irresistible target for political cartoonists. By changing the name, Congress hopes to avoid this cartoon peril. I mean, who cares if the project is good science and important? What's truly important is that our elected representatives maintain their sense of self-importance.

So today a project called the High Resolution Microwave Survey scans the sky for traces of extraterrestrial intelligence. This search should prove more fruitful than scanning the U.S. Capitol for traces of terrestrial intelligence.

Meanwhile, we beam out *The Brady Bunch* and *My Mother the Car* to the universe. If there is somebody out there listening, I only hope they catch an episode of Star Trek.

Now, remember those one hundred and fifty billion stars we were talking about? Listen, this is a great little theory. (I didn't invent it, but I can't remember the name of the guy who did. I saw it on TV so I can't even look it up.) Suppose only one out of one hundred stars has planets. This is supposed to be an extremely conservative estimate. Next, suppose only one out of a hundred of those is earthlike. Then suppose only one out of a hundred of those developed life. Finally, suppose that out of one hundred of those that developed life, one evolved intelligent life.

Calculating all those supposes means there are 1,500 civilizations in our galaxy. One thousand, five hundred societies that the Enterprise could visit and explore—conservatively.

Now, one last mathematical formula. On the average, twenty-six episodes of Star Trek were produced each year during the run of the original series. Therefore, if the Enterprise were to visit all the life-forms and civilizations in our galaxy, we could look forward to 57.6 years of new adventures. And that doesn't include reruns.

Advertising presentations are often called "dog and pony shows." They are little pieces of theater designed to build anticipation and excitement. The enthusiasm of the presenter shows that the advertising agency believes in the work they are presenting. If done correctly, this is a high-energy ritual that culminates in the client buying the ads that the agency presents.

Each client is different. Singing and dancing rarely achieve the desired result if the client is the marketing director for a mortuary.

Even the best presentations can go down in flames. Once,

while standing in front of a client presenting storyboards—thinking I was doing quite well—I was interrupted. "Excuse me," drawled our client as he leaned to the side and opened a desk drawer. "Does anyone else want an antacid?" he asked as he unwrapped a package of Rolaids he had produced from his desk. I hadn't wanted one before that moment. Immediately after, I needed one.

After ingesting the tablet, the client rejected our ideas and sent us back to the drawing board.

Timing is also important. Never give a slide presentation to three hundred dairy farmers who have just finished lunch. The combination of full bellies and a darkened room produces a reaction called sleep. I'll never make that mistake again, I promise you.

Perhaps my most difficult presentation was to Catholic Charities. Catholic Charities does great work. It feeds the hungry, helps get people off drugs and runs AIDS hospices. For this reason, our agency was glad to help them produce a series of public-service announcements.

Our client was no less than the head of the Catholic Archdiocese of Washington, D.C., His Eminence the Cardinal. Having grown up Catholic, I knew that a cardinal was one step from the Pope and the Pope is practically God. Cardinal Hickey is exactly what you would expect of a man of the cloth. He is pious, quiet, gentle and humble. Certain men have a presence you can feel. Cardinal Hickey had such a presence, and it demanded reverence.

My usual presentation style involves a lot of moving around, and I can be very loud. Once I get rolling, I tend to overheat. Hence my dilemma. Should I present in my usual style? Or should I become calm and humble? Most importantly, was there any error I could make that would damn my immortal soul for all eternity?

I looked to the heavens. And found the Starship Enterprise. Dr. Leonard McCoy had been in this exact situation.

Well, not exact, but close. While visiting a planet ruled by seven-foot giants, he discovered the tribal queen was pregnant. Complications put McCoy, the queen, Kirk and Spock on the run.

Naturally, while this group was on the lam, the queen began contractions. When McCoy tried to deliver the baby, the queen told him that none but a royal personage could touch her. He would be put to death if he so much as laid a hand on her.

McCoy would have none of it. He was the doctor and she was the patient. A baby boy was delivered on Leonard McCoy's terms.

So I introduced the cardinal to the dog and pony. I presented the storyboards with as much energy as possible. On one occasion, while describing a scene, I used the expletive "jeez." As it slipped past my lips, I bit hard. I had the good fortune not to follow this syllable with "us" and escaped undamned.

The cardinal loved my performance. He was a lively and appreciative audience. We sold all our ideas and produced a wonderful public-service campaign.

Apparently, most folks are fairly sedate around Cardinal Hickey. He found my presentation refreshing and loved the enthusiasm. A couple of days later, I received the coup de grâce. A priest who is close to the cardinal told me to consider the seminary.

I feel the presentation worked because the cardinal entered my world. Catholic Charities wanted advertising. They needed what the agency could provide.

If I had been there for an audience with His Eminence, a different approach would have been appropriate. But like McCoy with the queen, I was the expert here. And I handled it as I saw fit.

Bottom line? When in Rome do as the Romans do. But when Rome comes to you, do it your way.

I'm not sure how old Mick Jagger is, but it must be somewhere around fifty—a half century. Pete Townshend of the Who is nearly as old. The Beach Boys are the Beach Grandfathers. Elvis is dead, and he's still around. They all keep rocking right along. And they are putting our concepts of age and aging to the test.

Rock and roll is an obvious place to note this phenomenon, but it's evident all over society. For the first time in aviation history, for example, the flight attendants are older than the planes. It has become commonplace for corporations to bribe employees into retirement with special benefits packages. This notion of going docilely into your golden years to rest and relax has been blown to bits.

My father got married at seventy-five years old—not to my mother. She had passed away a few years earlier. He met his new bride dancing. They went bungee jumping on their honeymoon. Just kidding. They didn't go bungee jumping, but that really isn't a far stretch.

I had the honor of giving my father away at the wedding. Officially, I was the best man. As we waited at the altar for the bride, I couldn't hear the music. There was another song in my head—Frank Sinatra singing "Young at Heart."

Growing older has become the heart of the Star Trek movies. In *The Wrath of Khan,* when Captain James T. Kirk faces the finality of death for the first time in his life, it rejuvenates him. He feels young.

As the subsequent Star Trek movies were released, age always played a major role. It had to be. William Shatner, Leonard Nimoy and DeForest Kelley weren't getting any younger. The fact that three older gentlemen continued to be mega-box office attractions makes the point as strongly as any of the movies.

Age even becomes an inside joke. Bones talks of retirement in *The Undiscovered Country*. Yet in that same film, Kirk fights—and defeats, of course—an eight-foot alien, romances supermodel Iman, crosses a glacier on foot and saves galactic peace. Not bad for a guy a couple of months from cashing in his profit sharing.

It is often said, "You're only as old as you feel." But I'm a little more skeptical. If I want to figure out my age, I subtract the year of my birth from the current year. The resulting number is my age.

Plus I don't buy into this youth-culture stuff. Older is better. I know more. I'm more confident. I'm happier.

Youth isn't wasted on the young—they need it. Without their superior physical skills, they wouldn't survive to an age where they could enjoy the superior life skills that I now possess.

A close friend of mine plays in a rock and roll band called Mr. Right. I've listened to the bands he's played in for twenty-five years. This one is the best. He's not quite as old as Mick Jagger, but when he is I'm sure he'll still be rocking right along. Just like Kirk, Spock, Bones and, hopefully, me.

About the time I entered the seventh grade at Saint Joseph's School, Freddie and the Dreamers had a big hit song. It was modestly titled "Do the Freddie." An accompanying dance was imaginatively named "The Freddie."

The words to "Do the Freddie" went a little something like this:

> Are you ready, let's do the Freddie.
> Are you ready, gonna do the Freddie.

The dance was somewhat similar to a jumping jack. However, you would lift your left arm and left leg at the same time, then as they returned to the ground you would lift your right arm and leg. Repeat this motion and you were doing the Freddie.

Which is exactly what I was doing. I was rocking back and forth and humming the hit tune to myself. This was during recess at Saint Joe's. No one else was around at the time. I had found an unpopulated corner of the paved asphalt playground and was content to amuse myself with the new little ditty and accompanying dance.

I could have maintained this state for the entire fifteen minutes of morning recess, but my eye caught a glimpse of something that took me out my trance. It was a nun, Sister Mary Marie. And she was moving quickly toward me.

Back in those days, nuns wore a full-length habit. Long black dresses covered their legs and feet. Because of this, the only way you could tell how fast a nun was moving was the tempo with which her rosary beads swung from side to side. Typically, the beads would beat out a waltz. When she was in a hurry, her beads might tap out a samba.

Sister Mary Marie's rosary beads were playing "Wipeout." They swung wildly with each approaching step. Worse, I could hear heavy breathing from exertion. My God, she was running. As my gaze meet hers, I saw a red puffy face and steel eyes.

I continued singing but began to slow as Sister Mary Marie got closer. As the song slowed so did my dancing. "Are . . . you . . . read . . . dee . . . Let's . . ." I was like a 45 RPM record on 33. By the moment of collision, I had nearly stopped.

For a second that seemed like an eternity, we stood inches apart. Without warning, Sister slapped me hard across the face. It stung. "Don't you ever . . ." Sister began harshly, ". . . make fun of me again."

I was stunned, unsure how to react. Make fun of you? I stood dumbfounded with an aching cheek.

At times like these, my thoughts often travel to Captain Kirk. Surely Kirk would know what to do. Unfortunately, this incident transpired years before the network debut of Star Trek. Besides, I don't recall ever seeing a giant nun attack the ship.

There is, however, a moment in one episode that I believe is relevant. Beaming down to the planet Deneva, Kirk, Spock and Bones are attacked by group of men. As the men charge with murderous intentions, they yell to the landing party to be careful. Their apparent concern is totally contrary to their behavior.

The inhabitants of Deneva, it is later learned, are controlled by space parasites. Their actions are not by choice. They are not themselves.

I think something like this might have happened to Sister Mary Marie. Not that she was controlled by space parasites. But that there was something else happening in her life that made her interpret my dance incorrectly. Her actions had nothing to do with me. I was just there.

In later years, I might have considered that slap across the face as a cry for help. But at the time, I was just confused and did nothing. But I'll never forget what I did after Sister walked away and left me alone in my little corner of the playground. I did "the Freddie."

An old friend of mine once told me a truth about advertising. "A vice president in an advertising agency," he said, "is a person who can come into his office in the morning, find a single piece of paper on his desk and by noon have turned that piece of paper into a dozen problems."

I fear this is the rule in business rather than the exception. It seems every workplace has at least one of these types. This person is easy to spot. Look for an ambitious go-getter who specializes in discovering the downside of any situation. And, of course, someone who is constantly second-guessing the decisions of others.

As terrible as this sounds, most corporations reward this type of behavior. It's sick. Get two of these guys in one room, and decision-making gets so convoluted everyone ends up with their underwear on their heads. If this seems unlikely, go to work for a large corporation. Bring extra underwear.

Yes, I have met this animal—unfortunately, never in season with the proper ammunition. For now, the names will be withheld to protect the guilty.

No wonder I love Star Trek. Each week a problem arises. Each week James T. Kirk uses his talents and the talents of his crew to find an effective solution. Rarely do the captain and crew *cause* a problem.

One of the major reasons for this is that there is little second-guessing on the Enterprise. When Mr. Spock decides to cross circuit to "B" to handle a transporter malfunction, no one sends out a memo recommending he try three different alternatives. When Scotty readjusts the matter/antimatter valves, he doesn't have to follow a Total Quality Management program. Kirk gives his people the responsibility and the authority to get the job done. And they do.

Kirk solves the problems he can solve and delegates the problems that need to be solved by someone else. Simplistic, you say? Why not? Good managers usually know which problems to delegate and which to solve themselves. The real good ones support the solutions arrived at by their designated problem solvers, give 'em the benefit of the doubt and back 'em up.

Kirk does this every week. It's a lesson we can all learn from. Hey, there are already too many vice presidents at advertising agencies.

Star Trek never talks about food. Everybody on the ship eats, but what they eat is rarely mentioned. Most of the meals that are served are for visiting aliens. When we do catch a glimpse of the Enterprise kitchen in *The Undiscovered Country* there is something on the table that looks like bread dough. We never see what it gets made into, though.

I can understand why they avoid the subject. Every few years, all our beliefs on eating change. Not long ago, granola was considered the height of health food. Today, it's just another high-calorie menace.

Captain Kirk has a fondness for coffee. In one episode, his coffee is drugged with a substance that moves him into hyperspeed. Interestingly, coffee has the exact same effect on me even when it isn't drugged. In another episode, Captain Kirk orders a chicken sandwich and coffee from the food machine. Aside from reinforcing the captain's love of caffeine (he can't possibly drink decaf, can he?), it also means he's no vegetarian. I'm sure there are vegetarians on the ship. Enough hints have been dropped that it is fairly certain that Spock is one.

The only other big eater on any of the shows is Counselor Deanna Troi of *The Next Generation*, who is nearly a chocoholic. It's no surprise chocolate survives through the centuries. I'm sure as long as there is humanity, there will be chocolate. It does strike me that chocolate is full of caffeine. So Troi and Kirk are kindred in an odd way.

One thing the Enterprise never does is pull up to the drive-through window at a fast-food restaurant. We can speculate on the reasons for this. Size alone would dictate sending a shuttle craft or some smaller vehicle capable of getting close to the take-out window. Eating out may not be a reimbursable expense on Starfleet trips. The food synthesizers on board might replicate Big Macs and Whoppers. Or just perhaps there isn't any junk food in the future.

Can the latter possibly be the reason?

Lord knows, if we were to remove junk food from our society our civilization would probably collapse. Aside from important contributions to diet, culture as we know it would cease to exist without Arby's or Kentucky Fried Chicken. After all, most first dates include a trip to a fast-food restaurant. Interfering with the mating ritual at this basic level could have serious effects on the future of humanity.

So, what culinary lessons can be drawn from Star Trek? Stay hopped on caffeine? Vegetarians are aliens? The chicken sandwich will be the food staple of tomorrow?

When I was a kid my father would say, "If you eat too much watermelon, you're going to turn into a watermelon." It didn't happen. If such a metamorphosis were possible, by now I would have turned into a pint of Rocky Road.

Pretty much anything you eat will keep you alive. In college I knew a girl who managed to subsist on popcorn and ice cream sandwiches. Maybe that's all Star Trek implies. It isn't what you eat, it's that you eat. Just make sure you have a little something. Like my Auntie Emma used to say, "Mangia. Mangia."

When I was a teenager, I had a bad habit. Actually, I had more than one bad habit. Then again, that's the nature of teenagers.

Let's start this again. When I was in high school I would answer every question with the same one-word answer. I would say, "What?"

Most of the time I had heard the question clearly. My "What?" was just a way to give myself more time to think of an answer. I did this unconsciously. A grownup pointed out my little habit when she become annoyed at repeating every question.

"I know what you're doing," she said. I was glad someone did, because I didn't have a clue.

What I was doing unconsciously is something James T. Kirk does purposely on many occasions. I was stalling.

James Kirk is the master of stalling. (Actually, James Kirk isn't the master of stalling. Any parent of a five-year-old at bedtime knows the real virtuoso of this art. But back to Kirk.) When the Enterprise gets into a hopeless spot, the Captain will usually find a way to buy a little time, putting off the inevitable until the very last second. And by then, he's figured out a way to make the inevitable avoidable.

He deceives and distracts while Scotty makes the necessary repairs to the phasers or the warp drive. By the time his adversary realizes what's going on, Kirk has the upper hand.

There's an innate problem with this behavior. While stalling may occasionally save your skin, it's a terrible habit. It shouldn't be used indiscriminately, or it will turn into a pattern of procrastination. While this is a great advantage if you're seeking employment at the post office, in most parts of life it causes problems. I know. It happened to me. The trick is to apply this skill only when absolutely needed. And to buy time only for a known purpose.

When Kirk stalls to give Scotty the chance to repair the transporter, he knows why he is stalling. He also knows how much time he must buy, because he gets an estimate from Scotty of how long repairs will take. This gives Kirk the parameters for working out his strategy. He knows exactly what he is doing. The action isn't open-ended.

This is different from telling your spouse, "I'll be ready in a minute," when you haven't even decided what you are going to wear.

On the other hand, if you are buying the time to finish a report, to double-check a fact or to sneak out and buy an anniversary present, use any possible resource. Kirk would.

Hey, you can't buy love. But you can buy time.

One of my first jobs after college was as a mental health specialist for the state of Illinois. In this job I ran a home and supervised development programs for mentally retarded adults. I also supervised the mental health technicians who carried out the programs.

Mentally retarded adults meet with a lot of frustration in their lives. Like any group of people, some handle it well and others cope poorly. As I was young and agile, the home I ran became a popular place to transfer the more aggressive cases. While this made the job more interesting, it also made it less safe.

Complicating my task was the fact that my section also became a dumping ground for problem employees. Many times, working with the employees proved more difficult than working with the retarded residents.

Although there were prescribed procedures for handling problems, this environment constantly produced new challenges. Bad behavior was contagious. When one resident would act up, it would upset others. The situation would snowball unless stopped. Confining a misbehaving resident to his room didn't seem fair to me. This would have the effect of punishing the roommate. As I said, the job was very interesting.

I developed my own solution to stop small problems from growing into larger ones. In the house was a large living room. Almost no one ever went into this room. It functioned mainly as a visitors' room. As we rarely had visitors, we rarely used the room.

I turned this parlor into a cool-down area. The small corridor that connected the living room to the rest of the house became no-man's-land. Or as I liked to think of it, the neutral zone, a buffer between the person who was acting up and the rest of the residents.

This concept was taken directly from Star Trek. The neutral zone is the buffer zone between the United Federation of Planets (Kirk's side) and the Klingon Empire. It also separates the Federation and Romulan space.

The neutral zone on Star Trek kept the peace for hundreds of years. In my case, a couple of hours of peace was the most I could ask for. But it worked. This little cool-down area gave folks time to chill out.

After I left the institution, I took this concept with me and applied it to other parts of my life. When I moved in with my girlfriend, I kept an apartment nearby, a kind of psychic neutral zone. I think it helped both of us from feeling too much pressure. I'm sure it helped me.

When I worked at J. Walter Thompson, the neutral zone was a Cantonese restaurant called Louie's. The king-sized drinks served at the small Rush Street establishment provided the necessary buffer.

If my mother had used this concept, it might have eased much pain and suffering. My sister Barbara and I are two years apart in age. I'm older. We fought like cats and dogs from the moment she was born. This drove my mom to distraction. Finally she came up with what she believed was the solution.

She tied my sister and me together at the wrist and pronounced, "Now you two are going to have to learn to get along." While this technique worked with Sidney Poitier and Tony Curtis in the movies, at 14 New Street there was a different outcome. The experiment ended in failure when my mother removed the bloody stump that had been my sister from my arm. Instead of learning to get along, I just dragged my sister into all the furniture. It was a massacre.

Mom untied us, tanned my bottom and sent us to our rooms. What we needed was a buffer to keep us apart. I'm positive my sister would agree.

We all need a neutral zone to keep our problems at bay, a place where we can cool down. I owe that revelation not only to Star Trek but to a group of retarded men who taught me an important lesson in life.

As a young man, I tied my mattress to the top of my 1962 Mercury Comet and headed to Chicago to find my fortune. My dream was to become a stand-up comic. Back in those days there were few comedy clubs and no cable television. To get the opportunity to perform in one of the few venues, a comic—unlike comics today—actually had to be funny.

Arriving in that Toddlin' Town I learned of a place called Second City. Many big-name comics had started there, and they ran improvisation workshops. It sounded right to me, so I went to Wells Street to sign up for classes.

Second City was set up like this: At the bottom were the first-year students. Second-year students were allowed to participate in the Children's Theater. After your third year, you became eligible for the Chateau Louise Company, a road company permanently stationed at a dinner theater outside of Chicago. Or you could make it all the way to the resident company. Resident company members were gods.

These deities had their pictures hung over the box office of the Wells Street theater. Never had I seen such humans. What I didn't know was that all these portraits were airbrushed. Every flaw and imperfection was removed. One of these portraits was of Shelley Long, who went on to fame and fortune in *Cheers*. I had never seen anyone so perfect in my life. Her airbrushed eyes looked down on me in all my insecurity. That picture scared the hell out of me. Later, when I discovered that Shelley Long actually had moles, I was the happiest man alive.

So I wrote a check and began classes. Standing onstage before an audience, even if the audience is only your classmates, is one of the few places in life where you can experience tremendous fear without being in any real physical danger. People's responses to this fear are illuminating. I watched a guy totally lose it, insult everyone and run into the Chicago winter without a coat. He could be still running.

Improv turned out to be the best thing I ever did for myself. I could always think on my feet, but the classes taught me to think *calmly* on my feet. I gained poise and confidence. I met new people, made new friends. I did not, however, become any funnier.

My career in comedy would end almost before it began. But improvisation became a skill that I carried with me for the rest of my life. Any business where conditions quickly change or unanticipated questions arise is a business where improv is an important tool. Advertising is such a business. So is commanding a starship.

James T. Kirk is the greatest improviser I've ever seen. Mr. Spock ain't bad himself. To this day, I am amazed at Kirk's ability to create favorable circumstances in the worst situations.

His battle with the gorn is a good example. He is locked in mortal combat with a creature that possesses many times his strength. The thing is nearly indestructible.

Kirk grabs a bamboo shoot, mixes together powdered carbon, sulphur and a little saltpeter, shoves a diamond down the shoot, puts one end of the shoot against a rock and aims the open end at the gorn. KABOOM, instant cannon.

The real strength of improvisational ability is its application to almost any situation. It is an attitude. The skill is understanding how to approach a situation looking for an advantage. It is recognizing and moving quickly to exploit opportunity.

While I studied improv at Second City, I became aware of other opportunities in my life. A friend introduced me to the world of advertising. I quickly realized that this was a world where I could prosper.

With a little help, I found a way through the door and got a job as a copywriter at J. Walter Thompson. I perceived an opportunity and took advantage of it. My improv lessons didn't turn me into the next Steve Martin. They did help me find a career where I could succeed.

We're getting kind of near the end here, and we still haven't talked about the most basic question of all. What is the meaning of life? For what purpose are we here? How does Star Trek address the largest issue of our existence?

Lots of philosophers have tried to answer that one. Lots of regular folks, too. Monty Python made a film called *The Meaning of Life*, and while it was very entertaining, it left much to be desired in terms of a definitive answer.

The Baltimore Catechism also tackles this issue. In response to the question "Why did God make me?" it reads, "God made me to know, love and serve Him in this world and the next." That tells you what to do, but it really doesn't say what life means.

At the opposite end of the spectrum, nihilists believe there is absolutely no meaning to existence at all. Eat, drink and be merry, for tomorrow we die. There are advantages to that point of view, but I see a huge downside.

A giant single cell attacked our galaxy in the Star Trek episode "The Immunity Syndrome." By the time the USS Enterprise encountered it, the cell had already destroyed one starship. Worse still, the cell was about to divide. If this was allowed to happen, the whole galaxy might perish. Kirk, Spock and McCoy came up with a plan to kill the cell. The plan worked and the galaxy was saved.

On the bridge, after the destruction of the cell, Kirk made an observation. The cell was like a virus invading the body of our galaxy. The captain and crew of the Enterprise had acted like antibodies and fought off the disease. Wouldn't it be funny, mused the captain, if the purpose of their entire existence had been this one moment in time? To protect the existence of the galaxy, just like our antibodies protect our existence.

When Kirk pondered the meaning of his life, he saw the big and the small. Protecting the galaxy was put on an even plane with the work of the smallest microorganism in his body. His existence and the existence of the galaxy came into balance. But more important, he saw a defining moment in his life.

Well, why not? One great moment can give a life meaning. Meaning, like gold, is where you find it. For many, this purpose can be found in family, in giving one's children a better life or in being there for someone you love. For some, it's collecting a complete set of refrigerator magnets from every state. Others find completion in giving comfort to the less fortunate. Some find it in duty to country.

Not everyone finds that moment or inspiration. But I think most of us do. It can be a monumental event or something small. It may come in an instant or slowly become clear over a lifetime.

Whatever meaning a person finds in life comes from inside. We each define our own purpose in life. Perhaps all our purposes are not as grand as saving the galaxy. But we all certainly have a reason to be.

There is a new addition to the Star Trek family. Unlike *The Next Generation,* there is no USS Enterprise in this spinoff. Instead, the location of this series is a space station near a stable wormhole deep in space. Created by many of the same people who now produce *The Next Generation,* the series is more a cousin than a direct descendent of the original series.

The show is called *Star Trek: Deep Space Nine.* I prefer the name a coworker came up with. Star Trek Lite.

Because there is no ship, the occupants of the space station cannot seek out new life and new civilizations. They cannot boldly go, or even go boldly, where no one has gone before. Basically, they hang out in a mall and hope that aliens show up. Hey, if you think about it, that's exactly what we're doing on earth right now. We spend a lot of time in malls, and many of us are hoping that aliens show up. Maybe that makes *Deep Space Nine* the Star Trek for the nineties. It just seems a little less filling.

I do, of course, watch *Deep Space Nine* and will continue to do so. Like a good steak, the show could use a little aging. It could also use a little more meat. Still, there's time for that. The lesson of *The Next Generation* should be applied here. Let's show a little patience.

There are some interesting characters on the series. The best news is the return of a Kirk type. *The Next Generation* broke Kirk into pieces—Picard, Riker and Troi are all fragments of James T. *Deep Space Nine* reassembles him as Commander Sisko. Sisko runs the space station like Kirk ran the Enterprise.

It's hard to believe this is the same guy who played Hawk on *Spenser: For Hire.* Then again, I never watched an entire episode of *Spenser: For Hire.* But whenever I was zapping by and would stop for a moment, this big, brooding, bald guy would be menacing someone. Now he's cool, intelligent, commanding, dignified and cut from the same cloth as my favorite captain. I'd love to see him take command of a ship.

In a way, *Deep Space Nine* is the real next generation of Star Trek. Gene Roddenberry and Gene L. Coon are gone. Roddenberry conceived the original series and *The Next Generation.* Coon created the Prime Directive and helped define the Star Trek universe. They were the Marx and Lenin of Star Trek. Maybe Marx and Lenin are the wrong guys to draw a comparison to. Communism was a bad idea. Star Trek is a great one. Besides, I don't believe Star Trek will ever fall. It's even possible Kirk, Spock and McCoy might outlive Lenin, Trotsky and Stalin.

Graduating high school seniors sometimes choose a class motto. At Enfield High ours was, "We do not know what the future holds, but we do know we hold the future." I know it's kind of lame, but we were only in high school. I favored the motto a friend had used all through our secondary education. It was a line borrowed from a popular TV commercial: "Better living through chemistry." In the case of my friend, it certainly was more appropriate.

So it is with *Deep Space Nine.* Who knows where it goes from here? With a little luck, maybe the show will develop the right chemistry to enthrall future generations of Star Trek fans. A little time and seasoning will tell. I wish them luck.

My favorite Star Trek ending was Kirk on the bridge in *Star Trek: The Motion Picture.* Millions of us had waited years for the return of Captain Kirk and his crew to the Starship Enterprise. And finally, there he was, bigger than life, sitting in the captain's chair, smiling at the successful conclusion of a brand-new adventure.

Sulu, sitting below at the navigators' station, turned and asked the captain for a course for the ship. "Out there," Kirk replied as he waved his arms. "Thataway."

With that, we knew there would be more. There would be a Star Trek II, maybe III. The adventure would continue. And we could all come along for the ride.

It was also a symbolic passing of the torch. Before Star Trek, the great America morality play had always been westerns. Gunfights, frontier justice and bandits who went "thataway" were the canvas for the philosophers of the twentieth century. When Gene Roddenberry sold Star Trek to NBC, he sold it as *Wagon Train* to the stars. *Wagon Train,* a popular sixties western, proved to be the vehicle that set the stage for the metamorphosis.

I believe science fiction will continue to be the vehicle of choice for American screenwriters and authors.

Back in the first few pages, I spoke of an observation that

set me on the course to write this book. I don't know when I started applying Star Trek to my life. It just happened.

I know I'm not the only one with this relationship to Star Trek. Millions of people across the planet have been affected, or infected.

I don't consider myself a Trekker, although whenever I see Trekkers they seem to be having a great time. I just happen to think that Star Trek was a terrific TV show.

When I've heard "experts" talk about Star Trek, they credit the hopeful, optimistic outlook of the series for its longevity. Maybe they're right. But I think it's more than that.

There are millions of folks just like me who relate Star Trek to their lives. I know this is true because my friends frequently work Star Trek into the conversation to explain their life experiences. The only difference between us is that I wrote down what I felt. Who can guess all the ways we've been touched? If you've read this far, I'm sure you've felt the same things. I've only scratched the surface.

But while the surface is the place where many episodes of Star Trek begin, this is my place to pause.

This isn't an ending. There's plenty more out there, thataway. Next time, I don't have an earthly clue what I'll tell you about. Hey, every day is a new adventure. Maybe I'll tell you the story of the time the planet was on fire when they beamed down on it.

If you believe that Star Trek has had a significant impact on your experiences, please relate your original tale to me at P.O. Box 53178, Washington, D.C. 20009-3178. Don't forget to include your full name and address. We'd love to hear from you.

ACKNOWLEDGMENTS

Thanks to Mike and Jim. Tessa. Terry and Cary. All the Marinaccios, especially David, Beth, Justina, T.J. and Amber. Michael Brennen, too. Most of the Muscos. Paul. Andy. And, of course, Jane.